WORKBOOK

EXPLORING EZEKIEL

AMIR TSARFATI
& DR. RICK YOHN

HARVEST PROPHECY
An Imprint of Harvest House Publishers

Unless otherwise indicated, all Scripture Verses are taken from the New King James Version®. Copyright © 1982 by Thomas Nelson. Used with permission. All rights reserved.

Verses marked NIV are taken from the Holy Bible, New International Version®, NIV®. Copyright © 1973, 1978, 1984, 2011 by Biblica, Inc.™ Used by permission of Zondervan. All rights reserved worldwide. www.zondervan.com. The "NIV" and "New International Version" are trademarks registered in the United States Patent and Trademark Office by Biblica, Inc.®

Italicized words in Scripture passages indicate authors' emphasis.

Cover design by Kyler Dougherty

Original cover design by Faceout Studios

Interior design by KUHN Design Group

For bulk, special sales, or ministry purchases, please call 1-800-547-8979.
Email: CustomerService@hhpbooks.com

This logo is a federally registered trademark of The Hawkins Children's LLC. Harvest House Publishers, Inc., is the exclusive licensee of this trademark.

Exploring Ezekiel Workbook
Copyright © 2025 by Amir Tsarfati and Rick Yohn
Published by Harvest House Publishers
Eugene, Oregon 97408
www.harvesthousepublishers.com

ISBN 978-0-7369-9065-3 (pbk)
ISBN 978-0-7369-9066-0 (eBook)

No part of this book may be used or reproduced in any manner for the purpose of training artificial intelligence technologies or systems.

All rights reserved. No part of this publication may be reproduced, stored in a retrieval system, or transmitted in any form or by any means—electronic, mechanical, digital, photocopy, recording, or any other—except for brief quotations in printed reviews, without the prior permission of the publisher.

Printed in the United States of America

25 26 27 28 29 30 31 32 33 / BP / 10 9 8 7 6 5 4 3 2 1

CONTENTS

How to Use This Workbook 5

1. Experiencing God's Otherness (1–3) 7

2. The Consequences of Failure (3–7) 21

3. Overstaying Your Welcome (8–11) 35

4. Top-Down Sin (12–14) 47

5. Failure Theater (15–19) 61

6. Just How Nasty You Are (20–24) 73

7. Blast Radius (25–28) 87

8. With Frenemies Like These (29–32) 101

9. The Turning of the Page (33–35) 113

10. Rebirth (36–37) 127

11. The Great Ezekiel War (38–39) 139

12. The Return of the King (40–48) 151

HOW TO USE THIS WORKBOOK

What should you look for when you open your Bible? How do you draw out the meaning from what you are reading? And how do you make it work in your life?

Over the years of teaching people how to study the Scriptures, we have refined the process and will be using the following fourfold approach to the book of Ezekiel as spelled out in this chart.

EXPLORE THE BIBLE YOURSELF

1. CAPTURE THE SCENE (What do I see?)

2. ANALYZE THE MESSAGE (What does it mean?)

3. COMPARE THIS CHAPTER WITH THE REST OF SCRIPTURE (How is it supported elsewhere in the Bible?)

4. EXECUTE (How does this affect my life?)

CAPTURE THE SCENE (What do I see?)

This is the observation stage. As you read the Scriptures, you want to examine the passage with a series of questions, including, What am I seeing? What am I feeling? Who is speaking? Who are the main characters in the passage? What is he (or are they) saying? Why is he saying what he is saying? When is this situation taking place? Where is it occurring?

ANALYZE THE MESSAGE (What does it mean?)

At this stage, you want to dig a bit deeper and see what you can learn from the passage. What teaching is present here? What instructions am I being given? What is the intent of this passage?

COMPARE THIS PASSAGE WITH THE REST OF SCRIPTURE (How is it supported elsewhere in the Bible?)

Our understanding of God's Word is always enhanced when we look to the surrounding context or parallel passages. There is much to gain when we examine comparable stories or teachings in Scripture.

EXECUTE (How does this affect my life?)

This is the application stage. Once we let the passage speak for itself and understand it, we're ready to search for any life lessons that might be present in it. At this point, we ask, What can I learn about God or Christ? What doctrine or principle is taught here? And how can I take these lessons to heart so they influence how I think and live?

With these guidelines in place, let us now begin our study of Ezekiel!

LESSON 1

EXPERIENCING GOD'S OTHERNESS

EZEKIEL 1–3

The people of Israel had fallen far. They had turned their backs to God, and they had done so with reckless abandon. As they shamelessly pursued other gods and the desires of the flesh, God grieved.

This wasn't anything new. Centuries earlier, during the era of the judges, the people went through cycles of rebellion and restoration—repeatedly. Tragically, they simply would not learn from the error of their ways. Each time they came back to God in repentance, it didn't take long for them to wander off again.

When the Hebrews were still relatively new to the Promised Land, the great military commander Joshua had admonished them, "Choose for yourselves this day whom you will serve, whether the gods which your fathers served that were on the other side of the River, or the gods of the Amorites, in whose land you dwell. But as for me and my house, we will serve the Lord" (Joshua 24:15).

But it didn't take long for the people to forget Joshua's words. With each successive generation, they descended deeper into idolatry and immorality. Instead of being characterized as a nation who served the Lord, "everyone did what was right in his own eyes" (Judges 21:25). Rejecting God and His ways, they made poor choices that led to unspeakable depravity and wickedness.

The people of Israel embraced sin so enthusiastically that there was no longer any difference between them and their pagan neighbors. Those whom God had chosen to be distinct—to be a witness to the other nations—had lost all their distinctiveness. The spiritual darkness was great, and so was God's anger.

This is the setting in which God called the prophet Ezekiel. While it was an honor to be chosen as a spokesman for God, the job assigned to Ezekiel was daunting. God warned Ezekiel what he would be up against, saying, "The house of Israel will not listen to you, because they will not listen to Me; for all the house of Israel are impudent and hard-hearted" (Ezekiel 3:7).

Not only had the people spurned God, but they had also forgotten about one of His most fearsome warnings made centuries earlier through Moses. Before they entered the Promised Land, the Lord told them, "If your heart turns away so that you do not hear, and are drawn away, and worship other gods and serve them, I announce to you today that you shall surely perish; you shall not prolong your days in the land which you cross over the Jordan to go in and possess" (Deuteronomy 30:17-18).

If your heart turns away, you shall surely perish.

Because God keeps His promises—including those that have to do with judgment—He had to follow through. God had waited patiently on the people of Israel, to no avail. Punishment was necessary—and imminent.

CAPTURE THE SCENE (What do I see?)

Using your Bible, answer the following questions.

1. Where was Ezekiel when we first meet him at the beginning of the book named after him, and who was he with (Ezekiel 1:1)?

2. What suddenly opened, and what did Ezekiel see (verse 1)?

3. What was Ezekiel's occupation, and whose hand was upon him, according to verse 3?

4. As the vision unfolded before Ezekiel, what basic description did he give of the four living creatures (verses 5-6)?

5. What clue in Ezekiel 10:15 helps us to identify who the living creatures were (see also page 25 in your copy of the book *Exploring Ezekiel*)?

6. According to verse 15, what did Ezekiel see next to each of the living creatures, and what additional detail does verse 18 reveal?

7. Does the rest of Ezekiel chapter 1 ever identify the wheels in verses 15-21? Why is it best to not speculate as to their exact identity and meaning?

8. What did Ezekiel then see in verses 26 and 27, and what did he say this was, according to verse 28?

9. In verse 28, what was Ezekiel's reaction when he saw who sat on the throne?

10. What assignment did God give to Ezekiel in Ezekiel 2:3?

11. How did God describe the people of Israel in verses 3-5?

12. What did the prophet then see in Ezekiel 2:9-10, and what command was he given in Ezekiel 3:1?

13. After Ezekiel ate the object given to him, what effect did it have on him (Ezekiel 3:3)?

14. What did God tell Ezekiel about his assignment in verses 5-7?

15. How did the vision end, according to verses 12-15?

ANALYZE THE MESSAGE (What does it say and mean?)

Using both your Bible and your copy of *Exploring Ezekiel*, answer the following questions.

1. Ezekiel has one of the more dramatic calls in Scripture. It begins with a vision in which he sees angels and other supernatural things he is unable to describe. Ultimately, he ends up before God's throne. What impression do you imagine the vision left on Ezekiel?

2. In light of the fact Ezekiel fell prostrate before God's throne, what kind of accountability do you think he felt for fulfilling his commission?

3. Ezekiel's task was difficult: Alert the rebellious people of Israel and tell them judgment was coming. In Ezekiel 2:5, God said, "As for them, whether they hear or whether they refuse…yet they will know that a prophet has been among them." Why do you think God wanted His defiant people to recognize they were hearing from a true prophet of the Lord? (For helpful insight on this, see how Romans 1:20 ends.)

4. In Ezekiel 3:7, God told the prophet, "The house of Israel will not listen to you, because they will not listen to Me." Even though the people wanted nothing to do with God, the Lord chose to send Ezekiel to alert them about the consequences of their sin. What does this tell you about the character of God?

5. In Ezekiel 3:17, God said to Ezekiel, "Son of man, I have made you a watchman for the house of Israel." According to Ezekiel 33:6-9, what was Ezekiel's responsibility as a watchman, and in what way would God hold him accountable?

COMPARE THIS PASSAGE WITH THE REST OF SCRIPTURE
(How is it supported elsewhere in the Bible?)

1. The prophets Isaiah and Ezekiel and the apostle John all had visions of God's throne room. Read Isaiah 6:1-2; Ezekiel 1:13-14, 26-28; and Revelation 4:2-8. What similarities do you find in these three descriptions?

2. What parallels can you find in Ezekiel 3:1-4, Jeremiah 15:16, and Revelation 10:9-11? Why do you think it was important for all three men to internalize God's Word?

3. What did Ezekiel do when he was brought before the Lord (Ezekiel 1:28)? When the prophet Isaiah "saw the Lord, high and exalted, seated on a throne" (Isaiah 6:1), how did he respond (verse 5)?

4. Both Ezekiel and Isaiah were prophets who loved God and were loyal to Him. Why, then, do you think they trembled so greatly in the Lord's presence?

EXECUTE (How does this affect my life?)

1. Every believer has a unique calling from God. Though yours won't be as dramatic as Ezekiel's, it is still important because God Himself has chosen exactly where He wants to place you for His purposes. For each of the verses below, write what you learn about God's involvement and calling in your life.

   a. Psalm 139:13-16—

   b. Romans 12:1-2—

   c. 1 Corinthians 7:17—

d. Ephesians 1:4-6—

   e. Ephesians 2:10—

   f. 1 Peter 2:9—

2. Every person whom God calls has a unique place in the body of Christ. Based on where God has put you, how do you think He wants to use you?

3. First Corinthians 12:7 says, "The manifestation of the Spirit is given to each one for the profit of all." Every one of us is spiritually gifted in ways that benefit fellow believers. With that in mind, answer the following:

   a. How have you been helped by the spiritual giftedness of others in your life?

b. How have you helped others through your spiritual giftedness?

4. God called Ezekiel to urge the Israelites to turn from their rebellious ways. Likewise, there are times when God will use us as vessels to speak to fellow believers who are struggling with sin. When it comes to admonishing a brother or sister in Christ, what does Ephesians 4:15 say we should do?

5. What insights do you gain from Galatians 6:1-4 about coming alongside a fellow believer who has been "overtaken in any trespass"?

6. Ezekiel's calling as a prophet required him to be a watchman to the people of Israel. According to the following verses, in what ways can we, as believers, equip ourselves to be spiritual watchmen to those around us?

a. Acts 17:11—

b. 1 Thessalonians 5:21-22—

c. 2 Timothy 2:15—

7. While we should not expect to be given a vision of God in His throne room, what are some ways we experience God's glory today?

CLOSING THOUGHTS

On page 33 of *Exploring Ezekiel*, we read this about Ezekiel and Jeremiah feeding upon God's words:

> This eating of the word of God is a poignant activity. It emphasizes to the prophets that the message they were carrying to the masses was from Him. It was a tactile experience to point out what they already knew mentally. For each of them, when the pushback may have been at its greatest, they had that scroll-swallowing moment

to remind themselves that these difficult words they were speaking were from God and were 100 percent accurate.

In this way, the prophets were emboldened so they could persevere in the face of opposition.

We, too, can expect to get a hostile response when we let Scripture direct how we speak and live before unbelievers. John 3:20 describes the natural response of those who love darkness: "Everyone practicing evil hates the light and does not come to the light, lest his deeds should be exposed."

While we prefer to be liked rather than disliked, we know that as believers, our goal should be to please God, not people. And as Matthew 5:11-12 says, not only are we promised reward for any rejection we face, but we will find ourselves in good company with the likes of Jeremiah and Ezekiel:

> Blessed are you when [people] revile and persecute you, and say all kinds of evil against you falsely for My sake. Rejoice and be exceedingly glad, for great is your reward in heaven, for so they persecuted the prophets who were before you.

LESSON 2

THE CONSEQUENCES OF FAILURE

EZEKIEL 3–7

Illustrations are a powerful way to get people's attention. They're great for communicating an important point or giving a call to action.

As we read through the Bible, we see that God is a master illustrator. He conveyed messages through…

- types or shadows (the Old Testament Passover lamb, which pointed to the Lamb of God at the cross)

- symbols (the seven lampstands in Revelation 1:20, which represent the seven churches in Asia)

- metaphors (in John 6:35, Jesus said, "I am the bread of life")

- analogies (in Psalm 23:1, David said, "The Lord is my shepherd")

- parables (such as the parable of the sower, or of the good Samaritan)

God made frequent use of these tools to convey principles or truths He wanted to impress upon people's minds. When you look back on the things you remember most from the Bible, ask yourself: *Were they communicated through illustrations?* If the answer is yes, chances are that's why you found those lessons or points so memorable.

One of the more graphic ways God spoke to His people through the ages was by having someone use actions to communicate a message. When the Israelites fled from Egypt and found their escape blocked by the Red Sea, God commanded Moses, "Lift up your rod, and stretch out your hand over the sea and divide it" (Exodus 14:16).

After the Hebrews finished crossing the Red Sea, God then told Moses, "Stretch out your hand over the sea, that the waters may come back upon the Egyptians" (verse 26). Moses' hand motions were meant to demonstrate God's power over the waters of the Red Sea and affirm His ability to protect His people against overwhelming odds.

In the book of Ezekiel, God spoke frequently to the people of Israel through actions carried out by the prophet. God commanded Ezekiel to engage in unusual yet highly symbolic activities, including lying on his left side for 390 days, then his right side for 40 days (Ezekiel 4:4-8), and shaving his head and beard (5:1-4).

Every object lesson conducted by Ezekiel was simple yet rich with meaning. God never wastes "words." The messages God intended to communicate through Ezekiel's visual displays should not have been missed.

Yet the people were so spiritually blind and deaf that they were utterly oblivious to some of the starkest warnings found on the pages of Scripture.

CAPTURE THE SCENE (What do I see?)

Using your Bible, answer the following questions.

1. What did the Spirit do to the prophet in Ezekiel 3:24?

2. What two signs would Ezekiel experience, according to verses 25-26?

3. What was the purpose of the second sign (verse 26)?

4. What reversal was Ezekiel to expect, and what was he to say (verse 27)?

5. What was Ezekiel to portray on a clay tablet (Ezekiel 4:1)?

6. What was Ezekiel commanded to do in verses 2-3?

7. What visual display was next, according to verses 4-6, and for how many days was the prophet to carry out the two parts of this display?

8. In the next object lesson, what was Ezekiel to prepare, and in what way would this concoction be defiled (verses 9-13)?

9. What warning did God give in verses 16-17?

10. Next, Ezekiel was to shave his head and beard (Ezekiel 5:1-4). What warning did God then give through Ezekiel (verses 7-12)?

11. What would God do to the people of Israel in response to their idolatry (verses 3-7)?

12. What one bit of hope did God communicate in Ezekiel 6:8?

13. What does verse 9 say this remnant will remember?

14. What does Ezekiel 7:27 reveal to us about the fairness of God's judgment?

ANALYZE THE MESSAGE (What does it say and mean?)

Using both your Bible and your copy of *Exploring Ezekiel*, answer the following questions.

1. We are not given much detail about God's command for Ezekiel to lie on his left side, then his right. But we do know the reason. God told the prophet to do this to "bear the iniquity of the house of Israel" (Ezekiel 4:5). According to Ezekiel 22:2-12, what types of sin had God's people committed?

2. One truth that is prominently proclaimed throughout the book of Ezekiel is that sin has consequences. What consequences do we find listed in the following passages?

a. Isaiah 59:2—

b. Romans 6:23—

c. Galatians 6:7-8—

d. 1 Corinthians 6:9-10—

3. In light of those consequences, how seriously do you think God takes sin?

4. According to Ezekiel 6:10, 13-14, what is one of the key purposes of God's judgment?

5. To whom does Romans 1:18 say the wrath of God is revealed against?

6. Read Revelation 20:11-15.

   a. What clues in verses 11-13 indicate that it won't be possible for any unbeliever to avoid the consequences of sin?

b. What will happen to anyone "not found written in the Book of Life" (verse 15)?

7. Bible commentator Charles Lee Feinberg observed that "in Scripture, God repeatedly extends words of warning and admonition in grace before He unleashes forces of destruction in judgment."* Why do you think we can rightly say that God's announcements of impending judgment are expressions of His grace?

COMPARE THIS PASSAGE WITH THE REST OF SCRIPTURE
(How is it supported elsewhere in the Bible?)

1. When Ezekiel spoke about the sins the people of Israel committed on the mountains, he was referring to their worship of idols in high places.

    a. In Ezekiel 6:1-7, what does Ezekiel say God will do to the high places of Israel?

---

* Charles Lee Feinberg, *The Prophecy of Ezekiel* (Eugene, OR: Wipf and Stock, 2003), 35.

b. Now contrast this with Ezekiel 36:1-15. What future promise does God make about Israel's mountains and hills in verses 8-10?

2. In Ezekiel 6, God condemned His people for their incense altars and idols. What do the following passages tell us about idols and idolatry?

   a. Exodus 20:3-6—

   b. Deuteronomy 27:15—

   c. Psalm 135:15-18—

d. Jeremiah 11:12—

3. In Ezekiel 7:3, 4, 8, 9, and 27, we read that God's destruction of Israel was because of the choices the people had made. He repeatedly told them, "I will repay you according to your ways."

   a. Read Romans 2:6-10. What will God render to each person (verse 6), and what are the two possible outcomes (verses 7-10)?

   b. What promises are made to believers in Psalm 103:10 and Romans 8:1?

EXECUTE (How does this affect my life?)

1. For the ancient Israelites, idolatry was a huge stumbling block. Instead of seeking the one true God, they would seek other gods.

   We may think we wouldn't be so foolish as to do that, but idolatry comes in many forms. Loving or wanting someone or something more than God is idolatry. What are some ways it is possible for us to commit idolatry today?

2. What does it look like for us to love God above all else?

3. No Christian is able to attain perfection—that won't happen until we are in heaven. We all stumble at one time or another. When that happens, what should we do as quickly as possible, according to 1 John 1:9? And what does God promise to do?

4. Why do you think God hates sin so much? As you answer, think in terms of the damage sin does to God's creation.

5. Jeremiah 17:9 says, "The heart is deceitful above all things, and desperately wicked; who can know it?" What are some ways that sin within our heart can deceive or delude us?

6. We may sometimes think that a hidden sin in our lives won't affect others. But why is it that all sin—no matter how well we hide it—ultimately affects our relationship with God and with those around us?

7. Ephesians 4:26 says, "Be angry, and do not sin: do not let the sun go down on your wrath." Why is there wisdom in making sure we don't allow negative emotions or sins to persist within our hearts?

CLOSING THOUGHTS

Sin is like cancer. When it's left unchecked, it spreads. In the human body, cancerous tissue invades healthy tissue, leaving the affected person in a downward spiral.

For this reason, we need to take sin seriously. We may think we can keep our sins hidden from others, but even the secrets in the darkest corners of our hearts are sure to contaminate our thoughts, words, and actions. And whatever sins we allow to affect us will inevitably hinder our interactions with others and especially with God, who searches us and knows us (Psalm 139:1).

When it comes to overcoming sin in our lives, we cannot do it on our own. No amount of self-determination will succeed, for one simple reason: It is not possible to bear good fruit in our lives unless we are abiding in Jesus. As our Lord said in John 15:5: "I am the vine, you are the branches. He who abides in Me, and I in him, bears much fruit; for without Me you can do nothing."

How much can we do without Christ? *Nothing*.

This makes clear the absolute necessity of abiding in Jesus and heeding Him.

What exactly does it mean to abide in Christ? Very simply, we're to stay or remain in Him. We're to avoid wandering off.

First John 2:6 tells us more: "He who says he abides in Him ought himself also to walk just as He walked." We're to imitate Christ, to follow His example. That is made possible only when we stay close to Him and keep our eyes on Him.

A big part of abiding is to "let the word of Christ dwell in you richly" (Colossians 3:16). His Word has a cleansing effect on us and informs us about how we're to live. The more we let Scripture permeate our hearts, the more it will shape us.

The rebellious Israelites in the Old Testament didn't start out as rampant idolators. Smaller sins, left unrestrained, became bigger sins. To the point the people wouldn't listen to God anymore, no matter what He said.

If you don't want sin to spread in your life, keep a close check on yourself. Are you abiding in Christ? Are you keeping your eyes on Him and letting His Word dwell in you richly? And are you walking as He walked?

LESSON 3

OVERSTAYING YOUR WELCOME

EZEKIEL 8–11

In Ezekiel's day, how severe was the spiritual adultery in Israel?

Bad enough that God said to the prophet, "Son of man, do you see…the great abominations that the house of Israel commits here…? Now turn again, you will see greater abominations" (Ezekiel 8:6).

The people weren't wasting any time going from "great abominations" to "greater abominations." It was as if they were rushing to outdo one another in their idol worship. God was clearly not welcome in their midst. In the face of such contempt, why should His glory continue to dwell in the temple?

By now, Israel's downward slide had persisted for many decades. Judgment was long overdue. But God had been exceedingly patient, sending His prophets to plead with the people and urge them to turn from their evil ways.

Why had God allowed the Israelites to defy Him for so long?

Centuries earlier, God had told Moses that He was "merciful and gracious, slow to anger" (Exodus 34:6). The Psalms testify to the slowness of God's anger as well (Psalms 86:15; 103:8; 145:8).

Roughly a couple hundred years before the time of Ezekiel, God commanded the prophet Jonah to go to the Assyrian city of Nineveh and warn the people of impending judgment. At first, Jonah fled in the opposite direction. He preferred to see the wicked Ninevites perish under God's wrath. God turned Jonah around, and the prophet did as he was told. Surprisingly, the Ninevites repented—and Jonah was disappointed. In prayer, he confessed to the Lord, "I know that You are a gracious and merciful God, slow to anger and abundant in lovingkindness, One who relents from doing harm" (Jonah 4:2).

When it comes to judgment, God warns—again and again. For generations, the people of Israel abused the Lord's longsuffering. Without a shred of guilt, they trampled on God's patience. At last, God finally told Ezekiel, "I've had enough. The time has come to remove My glory from the temple."

CAPTURE THE SCENE (What do I see?)

Using your Bible, answer the following questions.

1. What happened to the prophet in Ezekiel 8:3, and where was he taken?

2. In verse 6, what did God tell Ezekiel to look for?

3. What did Ezekiel see in…

   a. verse 5?

b. verse 10?

c. verse 14?

d. verse 16?

4. What attitude did the people have regarding the Lord, according to verse 12?

5. In verse 18, how did God say He would respond to His wayward people?

6. In Ezekiel 9:3, where did the Lord's glory rise up from, and where did it go?

7. What mission did God give to the man with pen and ink, and what were the men who carried weapons to do (Ezekiel 9:3-5)?

8. What were the men with weapons to do when they encountered a person who had been marked (verse 6)? What were they to do to everyone else (verses 6-7)?

9. What did Ezekiel say to God in verse 8, and how did God respond in verse 9?

10. Where did the glory of the Lord move to in Ezekiel 10:4? From where did the glory of the Lord depart in verse 18, and where did it pause in verse 19?

11. Who did God command Ezekiel to prophesy against in Ezekiel 11:2-4?

12. In the book *Exploring Ezekiel*, on page 66, we read this about the men in Ezekiel 11:2-4:

> It was their self-sufficient, "We've got this on our own, so who needs God?" attitude that was so grating to the Lord. Not only did these men believe this lie, but they were in a position to deceive the rest of the city into believing they were perfectly fine to just keep doing what they were doing. These men were liars of the most heinous kind.

What words of warning did God give to these men in verses 7-10?

13. After God warned that He would disperse the people in judgment, what assurance did He give them in verse 16 (see also page 67 in your copy of *Exploring Ezekiel*)?

14. What promise did God give to the soon-to-be exiles in verse 17?

15. And what further promise did God give in verses 19-20 to those who would abandon their abominations?

ANALYZE THE MESSAGE (What does it say and mean?)

Using both your Bible and your copy of *Exploring Ezekiel,* answer the following questions.

1. In Ezekiel chapter 8, God shows His prophet four different abominations being committed by the people of Israel. This includes an idolatrous image (verse 5), idolatrous wall art in the temple (verses 10-11), women weeping for Tammuz, a Babylonian god (verse 14), and a group of men engaged in sun worship (verse 16).

   Then in verse 18, God says, "Therefore I also will act in fury. My eye will not spare nor will I have pity; and though they cry in My ears with a loud voice, I will not hear them."

   a. Based on what you read about the people of Israel in Ezekiel chapter 8, what words would you use to describe their character?

   b. What words would you use to describe God's character, based on His response to the people's actions?

2. In Ezekiel 8–11, we read about a major transition in God's dealings with His people. He determines it is time to remove His glory from their presence. Note the stages in which this took place:

   - Ezekiel 9:3; 10:4—God's glory moves from between the wings of the cherub on the mercy seat to the threshold of the temple.

   - Ezekiel 10:18-19—His glory moves from the threshold to the East Gate.

- Ezekiel 11:22-23—His glory departs from the East Gate and moves to the Mount of Olives outside the city walls of Jerusalem.

God's glory will return to a future temple during Christ's millennial kingdom on Earth. What does the prophet say will happen, according to Ezekiel 43:2-7?

COMPARE THIS PASSAGE WITH THE REST OF SCRIPTURE
(How is it supported elsewhere in the Bible?)

1. In Ezekiel 8, God revealed to the prophet some examples of the detestable idol worship the Israelites engaged in. What command had God given to His people long before this in Exodus 20:3-6?

2. Read Exodus 34:14 and Deuteronomy 6:15. For what reason did God prohibit idolatry?

3. In Psalm 115:4-7, what did God say about idols, and in verse 8, what did He say about those who make idols?

4. What did God warn would happen to those who worshipped idols, according to Deuteronomy 27:15?

5. In Ezekiel 9:3-4, which people did God say were to be given a mark? In Romans 11:4-5, what did the apostle Paul confirm happened in both Elijah's day and Paul's day?

EXECUTE (How does this affect my life?)

1. In Ezekiel's day, the people of Israel no longer welcomed God in their midst. What are some ways that we as Christians are guilty of leaving God out of our lives?

2. What are some of the consequences you personally have experienced in the times when you've allowed sin to come between you and God?

3. In 2 Corinthians 13:5, Paul wrote, "Examine yourselves as to whether you are in the faith. Test yourselves." Why is it good for us to examine our hearts frequently even though we have the assurance that Christ has already forgiven us of all our trespasses and cancelled our debt of sin, according to Colossians 2:13-14?

4. What are some reasons we fail to be diligent about dealing with sin in our lives?

5. Sometimes we justify allowing sin in our lives by telling ourselves we aren't hurting anyone else, or by saying the sin isn't all that serious. Why is it dangerous to have such thoughts?

6. Read Hebrews 10:26 and James 4:17. Based on these passages, how do you think God feels when we sin deliberately, knowing that what we are doing is wrong?

7. What are some ways you can regularly and intentionally make an effort to invite God into your life?

8. Psalm 42:1-2 says, "As the deer pants for the water brooks, so pants my soul for You, O God. My soul thirsts for God, for the living God. When shall I come and appear before God?" Does this describe your heart for God? Where do you see room for growth in your relationship with God?

CLOSING THOUGHTS

We would fully expect the pagan nations that surrounded Israel to have no interest in God. But the people of Israel themselves? For many centuries, God had revealed Himself to them. He had done miracles on their behalf. And they had received countless blessings from Him.

Note the exhortation God gave to His people in Deuteronomy 6:4-9:

> Hear, O Israel: The LORD our God, the LORD is one! You shall love the LORD your God with all your heart, with all your soul, and with all your strength.
>
> And these words which I command you today shall be in your heart. You shall teach them diligently to your children, and shall talk of them when you sit in your house, when you walk by the way, when you lie down, and when you rise up. You shall bind them as a sign on your hand, and they shall be as frontlets between your eyes. You shall write them on the doorposts of your house and on your gates.

They were to love God with their whole being. To teach His words to their children. To converse about His instructions day and night. To place His commands where they could not be forgotten.

After all that God had done for Israel, you would think they wouldn't need this admonishment. A few verses later, God even went so far as to say, "Beware, lest you forget the LORD who brought you out of the land of Egypt, from the house of bondage" (verse 12).

But they didn't beware. And they forgot God.

We are all prone to wander. We're easily distracted. A lot competes for our attention. Which is why we need to be intentional about remembering God.

In Psalm 16:8, David wrote, "I have set the LORD always before me; because He is at my right hand I shall not be moved" (or "shaken," as the NASB puts it).

That's the key to remaining steadfast in our relationship with God. When we are deliberate about setting Him before us, we will not be shaken.

LESSON 4

TOP-DOWN SIN

EZEKIEL 12–14

Proverbs 11:14 says, "Where there is no counsel, the people fall." That's exactly what happened to the nation of Israel after Solomon's reign ended and the kingdom split into two. Successive generations of kings, priests, and prophets indulged in sinful pleasures and led those under their charge to do the same. Bad leadership gave rise to bad followers.

You may have heard the idiom "a fish rots from the head down." When leaders are wicked and immoral, inevitably, their influence will corrupt those under them. They end up doing grave harm, leading people astray. Going back to the book of Proverbs, we read that "when the wicked are multiplied, transgression increases" (29:16).

This points out the importance of good leadership. It also tells us that those who lead others bear great responsibility. God will hold them accountable for anyone they mislead by their wrong words and actions.

The bad kings, priests, and prophets in both the northern and southern kingdoms could not plead ignorance. God had made His instructions clear to them.

To kings, He had said, "When he sits on the throne of his kingdom...he shall write for himself a copy of this law in a book...that he may not turn aside from the commandment to the right hand or to the left" (Deuteronomy 17:18, 20).

To priests, the Lord had said, "They shall be holy to their God and not profane the name of their God" (Leviticus 21:6).

And to prophets like Ezekiel, the Lord had said, "You must speak My words to them" (Ezekiel 2:7). They were to proclaim God's words, not their own. Any prophet who said, "Let us go after other gods...and let us serve them" was to be spurned and ignored (verse 3).

In Ezekiel chapters 12–14, God rebuked those in positions of authority for their rejection of Him and their bad leadership. He also addressed the people for their misbehavior. While the kings, priests, and prophets were responsible for leading people away from God, the people were accountable for their own sins. Everyone should have known better. And to everyone, judgment was coming.

CAPTURE THE SCENE (What do I see?)

Using your Bible, answer the following questions.

1. How did God describe the people of Judah in Ezekiel 12:1?

2. Who would try to escape the Babylonian invaders, according to verse 12? (You'll find the identity of this person on page 74 of *Exploring Ezekiel*.)

3. What does verse 13 say would happen when this person attempted to escape?

4. In verses 14 and 15, what did God say He would do to "all who are around" the prince and "all his troops"?

5. Read Ezekiel 12:16. Would God have everyone taken captive? For what reason would God do this?

6. In verse 24, what did God say would stop?

7. What did God promise in verses 25 and 28?

8. Who was Ezekiel to prophesy against, according to Ezekiel 13:1?

9. What did God say the deceptive prophets were guilty of doing (verses 6, 10, and 22)?

10. In Ezekiel 14:3, what did God say the elders of Israel had been doing?

11. In verse 5, what did God say had "estranged" the people from Him?

12. In verse 6, what plea did God give?

13. In verse 8, what did God say He would do to those who didn't comply?

14. Give a brief summary of the judgments God said He would send upon the unfaithful in Ezekiel 14:12-21.

15. What word of hope did God give in verse 22?

ANALYZE THE MESSAGE (What does it say and mean?)

Using both your Bible and your copy of *Exploring Ezekiel*, answer the following questions.

1. The situation in Jerusalem was perilous. The Babylonian army posed a threat. There were two kinds of prophets: Those who proclaimed judgment, and those who said everything would be okay.

    a. For what reasons is it likely the people preferred to listen to the deceiving prophets?

    b. What evidences do you think the people should have noticed that indicated they would not be spared from judgment?

2. What are some reasons that might explain why the foolish prophets would have been willing to lie to the people? (You'll find one answer on page 78 of *Exploring Ezekiel*.)

3. In Ezekiel 13:9, what three things did God say would *not* happen to the wicked prophets in Israel? Why do you think God imposed especially severe judgment on false prophets?

4. The elders of Israel were responsible for the spiritual welfare of the people. But what had they set up in their hearts, according to Ezekiel 14:3? What was the result of the condition of their hearts (verses 4-5)?

5. What would the righteous prayers of Noah, Daniel, and Job not have been able to do (see page 83)? What does this communicate to us about the spiritual state of the people of Israel?

6. Why should we find assurance in the fact God promises to follow through when He warns the wicked that judgment is imminent?

COMPARE THIS PASSAGE WITH THE REST OF SCRIPTURE
(How is it supported elsewhere in the Bible?)

1. In 2 Kings 25, we read the fulfillment of the prophecies given in Ezekiel 12:1-14. Read 2 Kings 25:1-12, and note below what happened:

   a. Verse 1—

   b. Verse 3—

   c. Verse 4—

   d. Verse 5—

e. Verse 6—

f. Verse 7—

g. Verses 8-10—

h. Verse 11—

i. Verse 12—

2. In the following passages, what does the Bible tell us about false prophets and teachers?

a. Jeremiah 23:16—

b. Matthew 7:15—

c. 2 Peter 2:1, 3—

d. Jude 12-13—

e. Jude 16—

EXECUTE (How does this affect my life?)

1. What does Acts 17:11 say that the believers in Berea did to safeguard themselves from false teaching?

2. For what reason was Scripture given to us, according to Psalm 119:105?

3. Read John 14:21. In what way do we show our love for God?

4. First Peter 2:1-2 says, "Therefore, laying aside all malice, all deceit, hypocrisy, envy, and all evil speaking, as newborn babes, desire the pure milk of the word, that you may grow." Do you think it is possible for a Christian to grow spiritually at the same time he or she clings to sinful attitudes and behaviors? Why or why not?

5. What does James 1:22 say we do to ourselves when we hear God's Word but fail to apply it?

6. What are some examples of harmful ideas and teachings that are being promoted in Christian circles today?

7. List three or four ways you are currently investing in your spiritual growth and maturity to protect yourself from negative influences. Where do you see room for improvement?

CLOSING THOUGHTS

When God made Abraham's descendants His chosen people, He didn't do so based on anything that would make them deserving of His grace and mercy. God acted out of the goodness of His heart. Their status as a chosen people was not earned. Rather, it was freely given out of love.

However, as God's people, they were given a weighty responsibility. They were expected to represent Him to a watching world. With the Lord as their provider and sustainer, they had every reason to love and honor Him and to do what was right.

Yet even after the Israelites had experienced God's gifts and blessings, they turned their backs on Him and chased after the enticements of the pagan cultures around them. Because they didn't take their responsibility seriously, they brought destruction upon themselves.

Similarly, there is nothing we can do to earn the salvation offered by Christ. Titus 3:5 says we are saved "not by works of righteousness which we have done, but according to His mercy." This same passage goes on to say it is the Lord who saves us, it is the Holy Spirit that regenerates and renews us, and it is through God's grace that we "become heirs according to the hope of eternal life." Everything about our redemption is all of God. There is no effort or credit on our part.

But once we become believers, we're called to take our faith seriously. The New Testament repeatedly emphasizes this truth. We're to be as athletes who train diligently so that we will run the race well: "Do you not know that those who run in a race all run, but one receives the prize? Run in such a way that you may obtain it" (1 Corinthians 9:24).

Running to win requires athletes to say no to anything that would hinder their performance—not just occasionally, but consistently. And running the spiritual race well means saying no to fleshly lusts and impulses that will lead us away from God.

Let us commit to training well so that we finish well!

LESSON 5

FAILURE THEATER

EZEKIEL 15–19

The people of Israel had all they could ever want. The God of the universe—who had the power and resources to bless them in every way possible—had taken them under His wing. His presence was in their midst, with His glory residing in the temple. God had placed them in a land flowing with milk and honey. They had been given laws that would enable them to follow God's perfect design for righteous and healthy living.

The Israelites had the honor of serving and worshipping the one true God, of being the recipients of His attention and care. They had been granted the privilege of shining God's light to the dark cultures around them. God also revealed to them His plans for their future, plans that would be fulfilled provided they remained obedient to Him. And most important of all, God had promised that through them would come a Messiah who would save people from their sins and establish a glorious kingdom that would last forever.

God had given the Israelites the most meaningful purpose a person can have: to live as His representatives to those around them. As implied in Ezekiel 15:1-5, as long as the Israelites were like a vine that bore fruit, they were useful.

But the nation had become spiritually barren, like dead wood. Therefore, they had become useless to God. Because the people had repeatedly rejected the Lord, He said, "Like the wood of the vine among the trees of the forest, which I have given to the fire for fuel, so I will give up the inhabitants of

Jerusalem, and I will set My face against them...Thus I will make the land desolate, because they have persisted in unfaithfulness" (verses 6-8).

God desired righteous fruit, yet the people bore unrighteous fruit. They had completely abandoned the very purpose the Lord had given to them as His vine.

In full view of the surrounding nations, the Israelites were dragging God's name through the mud. To make it clear to everyone—back then and for all time—just how bad things had gotten, God listed in Ezekiel 15–19 the sins that had made judgment necessary. In this way, God showed for all time that His people clearly deserved His wrath, and that He was perfectly just in punishing them.

CAPTURE THE SCENE (What do I see?)

Using your Bible, answer the following questions.

1. What point did God make about Israel in Ezekiel 15:2-5? (For insight on this, see pages 89-90 in your copy of *Exploring Ezekiel*.)

2. How did God say He would deal with Israel's spiritual adultery (verses 6-8)?

3. In Ezekiel 16:5, God told Israel, "No eye pitied you…to have compassion on you; but you were thrown out into the open field, when you yourself were loathed on the day you were born." How did God respond to Israel's desolate state (verses 6-12), and what does this say about God's feelings toward Israel?

4. In spite of God's care, what did Israel end up doing (verses 15-16)?

5. As the people sought to please every idol imaginable, what wicked practice did they engage in (verses 20-21)?

6. How extensive was Israel's idolatry (verses 24-25)?

7. To whom did God compare the Israelites in Ezekiel 16:46-51 as He described the depths of their abominations?

8. Even so, what pledge did God make in verses 60-63?

9. In Ezekiel 17:24, we read, "All the trees of the field shall know that I, the LORD, have brought down the high tree and exalted the low tree, dried up the green tree and made the dry tree flourish; I, the LORD, have spoken and have done it." What insight are we given about this passage on page 96 of *Exploring Ezekiel*?

10. What do we learn about the fairness of God's justice in Ezekiel 18:19-20?

11. When the people accused God of not being fair, what did He tell them (verse 29)?

12. What did God say would happen to those who repented from their transgressions (verses 30-32)?

13. How had Judah started out, according to the description in Ezekiel 19:10-11?

14. But because of idolatry, how did Judah end up (verses 12-14)?

ANALYZE THE MESSAGE (What does it say and mean?)

Using both your Bible and your copy of *Exploring Ezekiel,* answer the following questions.

1. In Ezekiel 15, God described Israel as an unfruitful vine—as barren wood. In what ways did God describe the uselessness of this wood in verses 2-5?

2. In Ezekiel chapter 16, God portrayed Israel as an unfaithful wife. How does verse 14 describe the result of God's love for Israel? After Israel committed spiritual adultery, what did God say to her in verse 30?

3. What does the fact God compared Israel to Sodom and Gomorrah reveal about the extent of her sin (Ezekiel 16:44-59)?

4. Read Ezekiel 18:20, then 18:30. Based on these passages, how can we know with certainty that God judges fairly?

COMPARE THIS PASSAGE WITH THE REST OF SCRIPTURE
(How is it supported elsewhere in the Bible?)

1. In Ezekiel 15:1-5, God said that a vine that no longer bears fruit is worthless and is good for nothing except being thrown into a fire. What somewhat similar statement did Jesus make in John 15:1-6?

2. Read Isaiah 5:1-7.

    a. What had God hoped His vineyard would produce, and what did it produce instead?

    b. What question does God ask in verse 4, and what is the implied answer?

    c. Because the vineyard produced wild and useless grapes, what would God do to it (verses 5-6)?

3. Even after God's people had sinned grievously against Him, in Ezekiel 16:60-63, He promised a new and everlasting covenant to them. In what ways do we see God's faithfulness to Israel expressed in the following passages?

   a. Leviticus 26:44—

   b. Psalm 94:14—

   c. Jeremiah 33:25-26—

EXECUTE (How does this affect my life?)

1. Even as Israel faced judgment, God affirmed He would bring restoration someday. In what ways does God's justice and love serve as an example for how we are to interact with others?

2. Though Israel had been unfaithful to God, the Lord was still faithful to His people. In the times when you've neglected or disobeyed God, how has He shown His faithfulness to you?

3. As you witness how God rebukes yet still cares about His people, what insights or encouragement do you gain about the kind of Father and Shepherd He is and will be for you?

4. If the people of Israel had borne fruit, God would have been able to use them to have a positive impact on the evil nations around them. Considering where God has placed you in life, who might God want you to have a positive influence on?

5. When God warned of judgment, His people accused Him of being unfair. In what ways do we sometimes accuse God of being unfair?

6. Scripture makes it clear God is never unfair. In what ways does this give you assurance and confidence?

7. Based on what you have learned so far in Ezekiel, how has your appreciation for God increased?

CLOSING THOUGHTS

Though the people of Israel had abandoned God, the Lord would not abandon them. Yes, He would judge and punish them. But He would also keep His everlasting covenant with them. He would reestablish them in the future. In the end, this would cause them to know that He is the Lord.

In all of God's dealings with His people, two truths shine brightly: God is just, and He is faithful. We can always trust Him to do what is right. Always!

The same truths evidenced in God's relationship with His people Israel are evidenced in His dealings with us today. We can be sure of that because God never changes. From everlasting to everlasting, He is God. Which means He is always just, and He is always faithful.

Why did God provide such a lengthy record of His interactions with Israel in Scripture? Why did He go into such great detail about Israel's rejection of Him and sins against Him? At first glance, we might assume the many accounts of Israel's spiritual adultery don't have much relevance to us. But there is much we can learn from what has been preserved on the pages of the Old Testament.

In Romans 15:4, Paul wrote, "Whatever things were written before were written for our learning, that we through the patience and comfort of the Scriptures might have hope." We benefit greatly from seeing God at work in the past, for it informs us of how God will work today and in the future. We see God's character and His ways on full display, which helps us to have a better understanding of God—and to know how truly wonderful He is.

LESSON 6

JUST HOW NASTY YOU ARE

EZEKIEL 20–24

Sin has a way of distorting our perspective. When we harbor sin in our lives, we do not see clearly. We may try to convince ourselves that isn't the case, but it is. Sin blurs the lens through which we see everything in life—including how we view God.

That's what had happened to the elders of ancient Israel. In Ezekiel 20:1, we read that "certain of the elders…came to inquire of the LORD." We don't know what they planned to inquire about. But they had "set up their idols in their hearts" (Ezekiel 14:3), and it was brash of them to think they could approach God. They foolishly assumed the Lord would willingly answer them. That's how twisted their perspective was. Though they may have tried to hide their idolatry from God, their unrighteousness was on full display to Him. He could see right through their act.

God told them, very directly, "I will not be inquired of by you" (verse 3).

It's not pleasant to read about the abominations committed by the Israelites. Their sordid deeds make for painful reading. But from them we learn many important lessons, including the futility of trying to hide our sins from God.

God is all-knowing and sees into every person's heart. There is nothing we can hide from Him. That can be scary to acknowledge, but living in full recognition of God's omniscience can motivate us to purity. Or at least, that's the effect such awareness should have on our lives.

So when we harbor sin within us—no matter how trivial it might seem—we should remember these elders of Israel. Blinded by the effects of their sin, they thought they could come before God. They were wrong. As Habakkuk 1:13 says, God is "of purer eyes than to behold evil, and cannot look on wickedness." Because God cannot overlook sin, it will impede our relationship with Him.

Also, no matter how hard we might try to keep our sin hidden to ourselves, it is sure to spill over into our attitudes and actions toward others. Inevitably, our wrong choices will affect those around us. Just as our love for God should motivate us to righteous living, so should our love for others.

With those truths in mind, let's see what we can learn from Ezekiel 20–24.

CAPTURE THE SCENE (What do I see?)

Using your Bible, answer the following questions.

1. According to Ezekiel 20:6, what oath had God made to Israel while the people were still in Egypt?

2. What request did God make of the people in verse 7?

3. What did the people end up doing (verse 8)?

4. How did God say He would respond (verse 8), and why (verse 9)?

5. Later, when God withheld judgment, what was the reason (verse 22)?

6. What ray of sunshine do we see in Ezekiel 20:37-44, and how do we know this doesn't refer to the exiles' eventual return from Babylon, but a restoration in the distant future? (For help with this, see pages 107-108 in *Exploring Ezekiel*.)

7. When God sent judgment through the swords of the Babylonian soldiers, what would be the result (Ezekiel 21:3-4)?

8. How would the Israelites who were already in exile in Babylon respond to the news about this latest siege and destruction of Jerusalem (verse 7)?

9. What did God command Ezekiel to do in verses 19-20, and which way would the king of Babylon end up going (verse 24)?

10. Read Ezekiel 22:6-12. In what ways had the Israelites dishonored God?

11. As God pronounced judgment, He condemned Israel's leaders.

   a. What were the prophets guilty of (verse 25)?

b. What had the priests done wrong (verse 26)?

c. What had the princes done (verse 27)?

12. When God searched for a righteous leader who could intervene before judgment came upon Jerusalem, what was the result (verse 30)?

13. Read Ezekiel 24:15-17 and pages 119-121 in *Exploring Ezekiel*. What point did God want to make to the people through the death of Ezekiel's wife?

14. What did God then say He would do to the temple (verse 21, pages 120-121 in *Exploring Ezekiel*)?

ANALYZE THE MESSAGE (What does it say and mean?)

Using both your Bible and your copy of *Exploring Ezekiel*, answer the following questions.

1. In Ezekiel chapters 20–24, we read at length about the destruction Babylon will unleash upon Jerusalem. To the casual observer in that day, it may have appeared that Babylon was simply conquering the holy city and its people. But who was really behind—and in control of—all that happened, according to the following passages?

   a. Ezekiel 21:3—

   b. Ezekiel 21:18-27—

c. Ezekiel 22:14-16—

d. Ezekiel 24:14—

e. Ezekiel 24:21—

2. In Ezekiel 20:9 and 20:22, God told Israel He did not want His name profaned before the Gentiles. Centuries later, in Romans 2:24, God told His people, "The name of God is blasphemed among the Gentiles because of you." Based on how the Israelites had behaved in Ezekiel's day, what incorrect impressions could the people of the surrounding nations have had of God?

3. Read Ezekiel 23:5-7 and 23:11.

   a. What do these few verses convey about the seriousness of Israel's adulterous betrayal of God?

   b. And what does the fact God searched for even just one leader to help turn the people around (Ezekiel 22:30) tell you about the extent of His desire for His people to return to Him?

4. When Ezekiel's wife died, God instructed the prophet to not mourn for her. What do you learn from Ezekiel's willingness to submit to God's will in such a difficult circumstance?

COMPARE THIS PASSAGE WITH THE REST OF SCRIPTURE
(How is it supported elsewhere in the Bible?)

1. God demonstrated His love to Israel not only through His special calling and His blessings, but also by warning the people to not go astray and worship false gods. What commands were given to the people in the following passages?

   a. Exodus 20:3-5—

   b. Leviticus 17:7—

   c. Deuteronomy 29:14-17—

   d. Joshua 24:14-15, 23—

2. In Ezekiel 20:40-44, God promised a distant future restoration of Israel. What do we learn about this special era in the passages below?

   a. Ezekiel 43:6-9—

   b. Zechariah 12:10—

   c. Zechariah 13:1-2, 9—

EXECUTE (How does this affect my life?)

1. In Ezekiel 22:30, God searched in vain for even one righteous spiritual leader to urge the Israelites to turn back to God. Who and what are some of the vessels or instruments God uses in our lives to encourage and exhort us to stay away from sin?

2. Repeatedly in Ezekiel 20–24, God made it clear He was the one who sovereignly orchestrated King Nebuchadnezzar to be an instrument of justice against Jerusalem. Read Daniel 2:21. Why does the truth proclaimed in this passage mean we can know peace no matter how chaotic our world gets?

3. Because the people of Israel were unfaithful, God was put in a bad light—His name was profaned. What are some practical ways we can put God in a good light when we interact with unbelievers?

4. For God to take the life of Ezekiel's wife for the purpose of making a point to the people of Israel was extremely painful for the prophet, but he honored God in the midst of his difficult loss. In what way does Ezekiel's example inspire you?

5. One significant lesson that runs through most of Ezekiel is that we cannot afford to become complacent about sin.

a. What types of sins can we easily become complacent about?

b. Why is it that complacency about "small" sins can lead to complacency about "big" sins?

c. What can we do to keep our guard up against complacency?

CLOSING THOUGHTS

Why did God's people fall into repeated cycles of sin?

We find a clue in the book of Deuteronomy. Actually, two clues. Before the Israelites entered the Promised Land, God said to them, "You shall *remember* that the LORD your God led you all the way these forty years in the wilderness" (8:3). A few verses later, God said, "Beware that you do not *forget* the LORD your God" (8:11).

Remember. Do not *forget.* Those two commands appear repeatedly all through Deuteronomy and the Old Testament. What ended up happening?

In Judges 2:10, we read that after Joshua died, "another generation arose after them who did not know the Lord nor the work which He had done for Israel."

Judges 3:7 says, "The children of Israel…forgot the Lord their God."

Later, in 1 Samuel 12:9, we read, "They forgot the Lord their God."

In Isaiah 17:10, God said, "You have forgotten the God of your salvation."

To Jeremiah, God said, "My people have forgotten Me" (18:15).

And yes, in Ezekiel 22:12, God told the people, "You…have forgotten Me."

They forgot—again and again. That's why the Lord urged them to remember.

Read carefully what Peter wrote to the believers in his day, and to Christians for all time, about the truths he wanted to teach them:

> I will not be negligent to *remind* you always of these things, though you know and are established in the present truth. Yes, I think it is right, as long as I am in this tent, to stir you up by *reminding* you…I will be careful to ensure that you always have a *reminder* of these things (1 Peter 2:12-15).

Remind, reminding, reminder. Peter made his point three times: I want you to *remember* these things! What initially appears to be repetition is actually emphasis.

When we make a diligent practice of remembering God and His truth, we are less likely to forget and to wander.

LESSON 7

BLAST RADIUS

EZEKIEL 25–28

You'll remember reading the following statement in the book *Exploring Ezekiel*, but it bears repeating here because it is so important: God only talks about other nations as they relate to Israel.

This helps to explain a major transition we have now reached in the book of Ezekiel. Up to this point, we've read about God's coming judgment upon His people Israel. But now the narrative expands to the surrounding nations. Ezekiel pronounces more judgments—but this time, against Ammon, Moab, Edom, Philistia, Tyre, Sidon, and Egypt. The reasons? Their sins, their rejection of God, and their hostility toward Israel.

Upon seeing Israel cut down by Babylon, these enemy nations and peoples would mock the Jews and assume their God was weak. But Israel's belligerent neighbors were about to find themselves on the wrong end of God's wrath as well. The Lord would make it clear to all that He alone rules over "all the kingdoms of the nations" (2 Chronicles 20:6).

When it comes to judging sin, God is impartial. He did not go light on the Israelites simply because they were His chosen people. Nor did He overlook the sins of Israel's enemies. As Jeremiah 27:6 says, God was about to give "all these lands into the hand of Nebuchadnezzar king of Babylon," for God "does not leave the guilty unpunished" (Exodus 34:7 NIV).

88 EXPLORING EZEKIEL WORKBOOK

CAPTURE THE SCENE (What do I see?)

Using your Bible, answer the following questions.

1. What was one of the reasons God would bring judgment against Ammon (Ezekiel 25:3, 6)?

2. What punishment would Ammon face (verses 4-5, 7)?

3. For what would God bring judgment against Moab (verse 8)?

4. According to the following passages, why was Edom deserving of judgment?

   a. Psalm 137:7—

b. Obadiah 14-17—

5. God judged the Philistines because of their ages-long harassment of Israel, which God described as an "old hatred" (Ezekiel 25:15). What did God say He would do to Philistia (verse 16)?

6. Ezekiel's proclamations against Tyre are extensive, taking up Ezekiel chapters 26–28. Give a brief summary of the devastation King Nebuchadnezzar wreaked upon Tyre (Ezekiel 26:7-14).

7. How would the nearby nations respond to Tyre's destruction (verses 15-18)?

8. What was Tyre's opinion of itself (Ezekiel 27:3)?

9. What would end up happening to Tyre (verse 27)?

10. How would the surrounding region respond to the fall of Tyre (verses 34-36)?

11. How did God describe the attitude of the king of Tyre (Ezekiel 28:3-5)?

12. On account of this attitude, what would God do to the king of Tyre (verses 6-8)?

13. How did God say He would deal with Sidon (verse 23)?

14. What would Sidon's destruction mean to Israel (verse 24)?

15. What word of hope did God give to Israel in Ezekiel 28:25-26?

ANALYZE THE MESSAGE (What does it say and mean?)

Using both your Bible and your copy of *Exploring Ezekiel*, answer the following questions.

1. In the following passages, what did God chastise Israel's enemies for doing?

   a. Ezekiel 25:3—

b. Ezekiel 25:8—

c. Ezekiel 25:12—

d. Ezekiel 25:15—

e. Ezekiel 26:2—

2. What common thread do you see running through all the verses listed above?

3. According to the following passages, what lesson would God teach to each of the nations He brought judgment against?

   a. Ezekiel 15:7—

   b. Ezekiel 25:11—

   c. Ezekiel 25:14—

   d. Ezekiel 25:17—

   e. Ezekiel 26:6—

f. Ezekiel 28:24—

4. What do all the above verses communicate about God?

5. In Ezekiel's prophecy against Tyre, we are given a clear and detailed description of the manner in which King Nebuchadnezzar and the Babylonian army conquered other kingdoms. Read Ezekiel 26:7-12. What do we learn about Nebuchadnezzar's military power and fighting techniques in the following verses?

   a. Verse 7—

   b. Verses 8-9—

c. Verse 10—

d. Verse 11—

e. Verse 12—

6. In Ezekiel 27, we read about Tyre's great riches and prosperity, which were a source of pride yet useless for protecting the people from God's judgment (see verses 33-34). What lessons do you think God wanted to teach other nations through His actions against Tyre? (As you answer this, consider Psalm 49:6-7 and Proverbs 11:28.)

COMPARE THIS PASSAGE WITH THE REST OF SCRIPTURE
(How is it supported elsewhere in the Bible?)

1. In Jeremiah 27:1-7, we are given a brief overview of all the judgments God would bring against the nations Ezekiel spoke of in chapters 25–28 of his book. Read what Jeremiah said, then answer the following:

   a. In verse 2, God instructed the prophet Jeremiah to put "bonds and yokes" on his neck. What do you think these implements were meant to symbolize?

   b. To which nations was Jeremiah to send words of warning (verse 3)?

   c. What did God warn these nations He would do (verse 6)?

   d. What would be required of these nations (verse 7)?

e. What does Jeremiah 27:1-7 reveal to us about God's sovereignty?

2. As mentioned earlier, God talks about other nations only as they relate to Israel. In Genesis 12:3, God told Abraham, "I will bless those who bless you, and I will curse him who curses you." What are some examples you've seen of this in either past history or today?

EXECUTE (How does this affect my life?)

1. Based on what you've read in Ezekiel 25–28, what words would you use to describe the attitudes of the people in the enemy nations that surrounded Israel?

2. What does the Bible say about pride and arrogance?

   a. Proverbs 16:18-19—

b. Proverbs 26:12—

c. Proverbs 29:23—

d. Romans 12:16—

3. Read the following passages. What attitudes and character qualities does God desire us to exhibit toward others?

   a. Romans 12:10—

   b. Galatians 5:22-23—

c. Philippians 2:1-4—

d. 1 Thessalonians 5:16-18—

4. Sadly, there are some Christians who believe the church has replaced Israel. But Scripture doesn't support that. God's covenant to Abraham was an unbreakable, forever covenant. In the New Testament, Israel and the church are always distinct entities. In passages about the millennial kingdom, we read that Christ will rule on His throne in Jerusalem. In Romans 11:16-24, God makes it clear Gentile Christians are grafted as branches to the root of Israel. And finally, there is Genesis 12:3, which says God will bless those who bless Israel.

   With all that in mind, what attitude should a Christian have toward Israel?

5. What are some practical or meaningful ways that Christians can show their love and support for Israel?

CLOSING THOUGHTS

One of the prevailing messages clearly proclaimed on every page of the book of Ezekiel is the totality of God's sovereignty. Whatever He wills to do, He will do.

Though the rebellious people of Israel did not want to be subject to God's authority, there was nothing they could do to escape their accountability to Him. Furthermore, none of the nations in Ezekiel 25–28 could alter His predetermined plans for them. As Isaiah 40:15 says, to God, "the nations are as a drop in a bucket, and are counted as the small dust on the scales."

While the fact of God's absolute sovereignty was painful for those who rejected Him, it is a source of comfort, assurance, confidence, and peace for those who love and obey Him.

Comfort because it means nothing will ever happen to us apart from God's purposes for us. We are secure in His hands. Our days were written in His book before we were born (Psalm 139:16), and nothing can alter His plans for our lives.

Assurance because it means we know God's plans will always prevail. In Isaiah 46:10, God says, "My counsel shall stand, and I will do all My pleasure."

Confidence because if God is sovereign, we can know with certainty that He is able to keep every one of His promises to us, and to fulfill every prophecy He has given. Everything God has revealed to us about the future will come to pass—including the incredible inheritance we have waiting for us in heaven.

And *peace* because if God is in control, we have nothing to worry about—nothing to fear. No matter how hopeless or chaotic this world becomes, God's plans will stand.

LESSON 8

WITH FRENEMIES LIKE THESE

EZEKIEL 29–32

Joseph was the eleventh son of Jacob—and the favorite. This provoked Joseph's brothers to hatred. It didn't help that father had given son a multicolored tunic that served as a constant reminder of Joseph's favored status. Other incidents occurred that infuriated the brothers to the point that one day, they conspired to kill him.

Reuben, the oldest, talked the others out of their evil plan. Instead, they threw Joseph into a pit. When some slave traders journeyed by, the brothers agreed to sell Joseph to them. That's how Joseph ended up in Egypt.

Joseph then became a servant of Potiphar, an officer of Pharaoh. All went well until he was falsely accused by his master's wife. Potiphar had Joseph thrown into the king's prison.

Through a convoluted set of circumstances, while still a prisoner, Joseph was brought before Pharaoh. The ruler had been deeply disturbed by a dream that none of his magicians and wise men could interpret. The Pharaoh's chief butler, who had formerly been in prison with Joseph, had remembered that Joseph could interpret dreams. Joseph was summoned, and God enabled him to interpret the king's dream.

So impressed and grateful was Pharaoh that he made Joseph the second-ranking ruler over all of Egypt.

Long story short, when famine struck the land, Joseph's brothers came to Egypt for grain. After more twists and turns of events, the family ended up reunited. So eager was Pharaoh to help Joseph's family and fellow Hebrews in Canaan that he told Joseph, "Bring your father and your households and come to me; I will give you the best of the land of Egypt, and you will eat the fat of the land" (Genesis 45:18).

While in Egypt, the children of Israel prospered and grew mighty in number. That is, until "there arose a new king over Egypt, who did not know Joseph" (Exodus 1:8). Out of fear, this Pharaoh—and the Egyptians—turned the Hebrews into slaves, "and made their lives bitter with hard bondage" (verse 14).

This frenemy dilemma led to one of the most stunning displays of God's judgment in the Old Testament—the ten plagues. Afterward, you would think that would have taught the Egyptians an unforgettable lesson about being on the wrong side of Israel. Evidently not, for in the time of Ezekiel, once again, God's wrath had reached the point He was ready to pour out His anger against Israel's frenemy.

CAPTURE THE SCENE (What do I see?)

1. What does the language God used toward Pharaoh in Ezekiel 29:3-5 convey about the extent of His anger toward Egypt?

2. How severe would God's judgment be, according to verses 8-15?

3. Who would ensure that Nebuchadnezzar defeated Egypt (verse 29)?

4. What further words of judgment did God pronounce against the Pharaoh in Ezekiel 30:21-24?

5. What additional insight can we find about the above-mentioned swordplay on page 151 of *Exploring Ezekiel*?

6. In what ways did God describe Assyria's pride and arrogance in Ezekiel 31:3-9?

7. How would God deal with Assyria—as well as Egypt—according to verses 10-14?

8. How did God explain His words about Assyria, and their meaning, in verse 18?

9. To what did God compare the king of Egypt in Ezekiel 32:2?

10. What did God say He would do to Egypt in verses 3-4, 7, and 15?

11. How would the nations respond to the downfall of Egypt (verses 9-10)?

12. Read Ezekiel 32:18. To where would God consign the slain people of Egypt?

13. In whose company would Egypt find itself, according to verses 22, 24, 26, 29, and 30?

ANALYZE THE MESSAGE (What does it say and mean?)

Using both your Bible and your copy of *Exploring Ezekiel*, answer the following questions.

1. What's remarkable about Ezekiel 29–32 is that all four chapters focus solely on God's coming judgment against Egypt. More words are spoken about the Pharaoh and Egypt than to any of Israel's other neighbors. In these four chapters are seven messages, all filled with pronouncements of condemnation and wrath. While the Scripture text does not reveal to us the reason so much is said about Egypt, what could the fact God had so much to say possibly imply?

2. Now that you have read Ezekiel's proclamations to Ammon, Moab, Edom, Philistia, Sidon, Tyre, and Egypt, what are some recurring themes you noticed about the reasons for God's anger against these nations and peoples?

3. Israel's enemies had rejected God. What had they put their trust in instead?

4. Can anyone escape accountability to God? Why not?

5. What do we learn about God's attributes and character as we read about His judgments against Israel's enemies?

COMPARE THIS PASSAGE WITH THE REST OF SCRIPTURE
(How is it supported elsewhere in the Bible?)

1. In Ezekiel 29–32, God had much to say about Egypt. The Lord also spoke about Egypt through the prophet Isaiah. What is the main point God makes about Himself and Egypt in Isaiah 31:1-3?

2. We find several striking similarities between the judgments of Tyre and Egypt. Let's look at some key ones:

   a. Compare Ezekiel 28:2 to Ezekiel 29:3. For what attitude was God angry at the rulers of Tyre and Egypt?

   b. Compare Ezekiel 27:3-7 to Ezekiel 31:2-9. What had the people of Tyre and Egypt placed their trust in?

c. Compare Ezekiel 28:24 to Ezekiel 29:9. What would people know after God had judged both Tyre and Egypt?

EXECUTE (How does this affect my life?)

1. In Ezekiel, God condemned those who put their trust in wealth and resources. In what ways is materialism a problem, according to Ezekiel 7:19?

2. When it comes to earthly riches, what did Jesus say was impossible (Luke 16:13)?

3. What exhortation is given in 1 Timothy 6:17-18 to those who have abundance?

4. It's not the possession of material goods that God condemns, but the mistake of putting one's trust in them. In Matthew 6:31-33, what does Jesus say our priority should be?

5. In Matthew 6:20, Jesus says, "Lay up for yourselves treasures in heaven." What are some ways we can use our time, knowledge, finances, and material resources to build up treasures in heaven?

   a. Time—

   b. Knowledge—

   c. Finances—

d. Material resources—

6. Notice that Jesus says, "Where your treasure is, there your heart will be also." That is, the location of your treasure indicates where your heart is. As you consider what you count to be your treasures, what does that reveal about your heart?

7. The people of Egypt trusted their riches to protect them and give them a sense of fulfillment. In this way, their riches were a stumbling block. What stumbling blocks around us have the potential to diminish our zeal for God and lessen our reliance upon Him?

CLOSING THOUGHTS

Had Israel and her neighbors put their trust in God instead of idols and power and wealth, He would have pronounced blessings upon them, not judgment. The direction in which they chose to aim their hearts made all the difference in the world between God's pleasure toward them versus God's anger against them.

It all came down to where their heart was.

Where is your heart? And where are your treasures? How you answer those questions will reveal the condition of your relationship with God. If you're honest with yourself, you are probably encouraged by some of what you see in your life. But at the same time, you are noticing places where you need to make some adjustments. Don't stop at merely acknowledging those shortcomings. Make a point of being intentional about figuring out solutions so you can grow more in your love for God.

God wants your heart. The beauty of giving your heart to Him and His kingdom is that when you do so, "all these things shall be added to you" (Matthew 6:33). God will provide your every true need, and you will experience a fulfillment that cannot be found in anything earthly.

LESSON 9

THE TURNING OF THE PAGE

EZEKIEL 33-35

"The city has been captured!"

Those were the words blurted out to Ezekiel by a survivor who had escaped the carnage in Jerusalem (Ezekiel 33:21). The Babylonian army had broken through the walls of the city, the slaughter had been horrific, and Jerusalem had fallen.

For several years, Ezekiel had served as God's watchman for the house of Israel. He had warned the people—repeatedly. He had urged them to turn back to God—repeatedly. And they had refused to listen to him—repeatedly.

As a watchman, Ezekiel had done all that God asked him to do. His was an arduous, thankless task. He had sacrificed much. But because he had been faithful to his calling, the blood of the people would not be upon him.

God said, "I have no pleasure in the death of the wicked, but that the wicked turn from his way and live. Turn, turn from your evil ways! For why should you die, O house of Israel?" (verse 11). In those words, we find deep compassion and grief. God had pleaded with His people, but they had left Him no choice. His holiness made it necessary for Israel's rebellion to be dealt with.

As Jerusalem was ransacked and burned, the people came to the bitter realization that Ezekiel had been right, and they had been wrong.

The fulfillment of Ezekiel's prophecies of judgment brings us to a major turning point in the book of Ezekiel. After so many pronouncements about God's wrath, it would be easy to assume the Lord would have nothing more to do with Israel. But as we will soon see, that wasn't the case.

Ezekiel 33–35 marks the beginnings of a transition. We read some wrap-up words of rebuke and condemnation. But we also read some early promises of restoration. In Ezekiel 34:11-12, God said, "I Myself will search for My sheep and seek them out. As a shepherd seeks out his flock on the day he is among his scattered sheep, so will I seek out My sheep and deliver them from all the places where they were scattered on a cloudy and dark day."

God the Shepherd had not given up. He would regather His people to deliver them. And He would stay true to the everlasting covenant He had made with them.

CAPTURE THE SCENE (What do I see?)

1. Read Ezekiel 33:4-5. Whose responsibility was it that judgment had come?

2. Because Ezekiel had done his job as a watchman, what assurance did he have (verse 9)?

3. What accusation did the people of Israel make against God (verse 17)?

4. How did God respond to their accusation (verse 20)?

5. What had the people done to bring destruction upon themselves (verses 25-26)?

6. In Ezekiel 33:31-32, we read about those who survived and ended up becoming the prophet's fellow exiles. How did they respond to Ezekiel's words (verse 32)?

7. What should the people have realized about Ezekiel all along (verse 33)?

8. In Ezekiel 34:1-6, who did God condemn, and why?

9. What was God's decision regarding the shepherds who had failed to do their jobs (verse 10)?

10. What promises did God make to His people in Ezekiel 34:11-16?

11. In verses 25-30, God describes what He will do for His people during Christ's millennial kingdom. What will His people experience during this time, according to…

　a. verse 25?—

b. verse 26?—

c. verse 27?—

d. verse 28?—

e. verse 29?—

12. Whose God did the Lord say He was in verse 31?

13. Ezekiel's prophecy against Edom is expanded in Ezekiel 35. While there is uncertainty about why God had Ezekiel prophesy again about Edom, what does God make abundantly clear in verses 7-9?

14. How will those who witness the destruction of Edom respond (verse 14)?

ANALYZE THE MESSAGE (What does it say and mean?)

Using both your Bible and your copy of *Exploring Ezekiel*, answer the following questions.

1. At the beginning of Ezekiel's ministry, God said, "Son of man, I have made you a watchman for the house of Israel; therefore hear a word from My mouth, and give them warning from Me" (Ezekiel 3:17). How do you think Ezekiel might have felt, not knowing what to expect and the degree to which he would be rejected?

2. Years later, on the verge of Jerusalem's fall, God said once again, "Son of man: I have made you a watchman for the house of Israel; therefore you shall hear a word from My mouth and warn them for me" (Ezekiel 33:7). This time, Ezekiel could look back on all that he had done. How do you think he might have felt this time around?

3. After many warnings, Israel didn't return to God. Does that mean Ezekiel was a failure? Explain.

4. Who were the true failures, and why?

5. In Ezekiel 34:11-16, God promises to restore His people. What does this tell us about His character?

COMPARE THIS PASSAGE WITH THE REST OF SCRIPTURE
(How is it supported elsewhere in the Bible?)

1. Ezekiel was God's watchman. What do we learn about a watchman's role from the following passages?

   a. 2 Samuel 18:24-25—

   b. 2 Kings 9:17—

   c. Habakkuk 2:1—

2. What charges do we find in the New Testament for those who are watchmen or overseers today?

   a. 1 Timothy 5:22—

b. Titus 1:7-9—

c. 1 Peter 5:2-3—

3. In Ezekiel 34, God did not mince His words when He condemned the false shepherds who had failed to care for the people of Israel spiritually. What similar rebuke did Jesus give to the religious leaders of His day in Matthew 23:13-15?

EXECUTE (How does this affect my life?)

Earlier, in lesson 1, we learned a bit about what it means to be a watchman. In the questions below, let's find out more about this vital role as we interact with fellow believers both inside and outside of the church.

1. From the very beginning of the church, watchmen have been necessary. What charge did the apostle Paul give to the leaders in the church at Ephesus in Acts 20:29-31?

2. Is the role of watchman for leaders only? What impression do you get after reading the following verses? Write down what each passage calls us to do.

   a. Romans 16:17-18—

   b. Colossians 2:8—

   c. 1 John 4:1—

3. According to Ephesians 4:14, what effect can false teachers have on us?

4. Why do people find false teachers so appealing (2 Timothy 4:3)?

5. How can we identify false shepherds and teachers (Matthew 7:15-16)?

6. Why is it sometimes difficult to identify a false teacher (1 Corinthians 11:13-14)?

7. In what ways have fellow believers helped you to have greater discernment about questionable ideas or teachings?

8. In what two or three ways can you help other believers around you to avoid being swayed by harmful or sinful influences?

9. What two or three destructive ideas and influences within the church are you most concerned about now?

10. In light of the constant need for watchmen in the church today, what do you feel a need to do so you're better prepared?

CLOSING THOUGHTS

"The LORD is my shepherd; I shall not want" (Psalm 23:1).

David recognized how great of a shepherd God was. Without Him, he lacked. But with Him, he had everything he truly needed—in abundance.

The people of Israel didn't realize how good they had it. They chased after other gods, wanting fulfillment but never finding it. The farther they ran from God, the more they sensed their lack. Which made them chase after false gods all the harder.

Next, David said, "He makes me to lie down in green pastures; He leads me beside the still waters" (verse 2).

Had the Israelites returned to the Good Shepherd, they could have rested. Instead, they exhausted themselves over futile pursuits. They sought happiness but could never find it.

David continued, "He restores my soul; He leads me in the paths of righteousness for His name's sake" (verse 3).

Idols and trusting one's possessions don't restore. They destroy, leading a person astray on the path of unrighteousness.

At the conclusion of Psalm 23, David said that because of the Good Shepherd, his ultimate destination was "the house of the LORD forever" (verse 6).

But because the Israelites rejected the Good Shepherd, theirs was a different destination—destruction and eternal condemnation.

The blessing of staying close to the Good Shepherd is that "goodness and mercy shall follow [us] all the days of [our lives]" (verse 6). What more could we want?

LESSON 10

REBIRTH

EZEKIEL 36-37

More than 60 times in the book of Ezekiel, God repeats some variation of this pointed declaration: "When you see this happen, then you will know that I am the Lord." In most cases, these words followed warnings of judgment. In others, they pointed to future times of restoration, some of which won't be fulfilled until Christ reigns on Earth during the millennial kingdom.

As it turned out, every single one of God's warnings to ancient Israel was fulfilled with perfect accuracy. This meant those who had heard the prophecies—then seen them come to pass—could arrive at only one conclusion: God really was God. The fact He knew the future so perfectly made it clear that His sovereignty was all-encompassing. If He said something would happen, it would happen.

This wasn't a pleasant truth for those who experienced God's wrath. But it woke them up to the fact that when God gave a prophecy, they could count on Him to fulfill it.

When it came to prophecies about judgment, that was a fearsome reality. But there was another side to all this. It also meant that when God spoke prophecies about restoration and hope, those promises were just as sure to come to fruition.

The devastation wrought by the Babylonian army left the people of Israel in a desolate place. Never had they experienced such hopelessness, such despair.

Afterward, the dust may have settled, but the uncertainty hadn't. The people were afraid. What did their future hold?

That's the question God answered from chapter 36 onward. The prophecies Ezekiel spoke were new and different. The people didn't realize it at the time, but some of these promises would have nearer fulfillments, while others would not happen until much later.

But regardless of when they would come to pass, God's intention behind these prophecies was to give Israel a glimmer of hope. He spoke of reconciliation. A cleansing. *A new covenant!*

God was telling His people He was not done with them yet.

The everlasting promises He had made to Abraham were still in effect.

And just as His prophecies of judgment had come to pass, so would His prophecies of renewal. Then they would know He was the Lord.

CAPTURE THE SCENE (What do I see?)

1. What does Ezekiel 36:3-5 say Israel's enemies had done to the land and cities? What attitude did these enemies exhibit?

2. What did God pledge to do to the surrounding nations (verse 7)?

3. What promises did God make about the land and people of Israel (verses 8-12)?

4. For what reason did God say He would restore Israel (verses 22-23)?

5. What promise did God make in verse 24?

6. What change will God bring about in the people at some point in the future, according to verses 26-27?

7. What kind of relationship would the people have with God (verse 28)?

8. Read Ezekiel 36:33-36. What clear clues did God give about who should get the credit for these remarkable changes?

EXPLORING EZEKIEL WORKBOOK

9. In a vision, what did Ezekiel see in front of him (Ezekiel 37:1-2)?

10. What happened when Ezekiel prophesied to the bones (verses 7-8)?

11. After the bones and sinews and flesh came together, what was missing (verse 8)?

12. What happened when breath entered the figures (verse 12)?

13. In Ezekiel 36:11, God identified the figures. Who were they?

14. What did God say would happen to the formerly divided nation of Israel (verses 16-17, 22)?

15. Who did God say would become the people's king (verse 24)? And for how long would this king serve (verse 25)?

16. What does Ezekiel 36:26-28 say about the kind of relationship God and Israel will enjoy in the future?

ANALYZE THE MESSAGE (What does it say and mean?)

Using both your Bible and your copy of *Exploring Ezekiel*, answer the following questions.

In the Mosaic covenant, God told Israel, "If you disobey Me, there will be severe consequences." If the people wanted to experience God's blessing, they had to honor and obey Him alone—or else.

Because Israel repeatedly rejected God through the centuries, some Christians have wrongly concluded—based on the Mosaic covenant—that Israel is no longer a part of God's plans and has been replaced by the church.

But that's incorrect. They're forgetting the Abrahamic covenant, in which God said His promises to His people were everlasting (Genesis 17:7-8). Israel's disobedience triggered only the consequences of the Mosaic covenant—it didn't negate the Abrahamic covenant. There was no way that could happen because Abraham and his descendants were not bound by that contract. When God unconditionally pledged to fulfill that covenant, Abraham was asleep (Genesis 15:12, 17).

Through the prophet Ezekiel, God repeatedly confirmed He still had plans for His people, and He would carry them out. How do we know this? Read the passages below, which bring us up to the transition point we see in Ezekiel chapters 36–37. Through these verses, we see confirmation that God's original promises to Abraham have not and will not come to an end. For each passage, write a short summary of what God says.

1. Ezekiel 11:17-21—

2. Ezekiel 16:60-63—

3. Ezekiel 17:22-24—

4. Ezekiel 20:33-44—

5. Ezekiel 28:25-26—

6. Ezekiel 34:11-16—

7. Ezekiel 34:25-31—

8. Ezekiel 36:24-28—

COMPARE THIS PASSAGE WITH THE REST OF SCRIPTURE
(How is it supported elsewhere in the Bible?)

The permanence of God's covenant with Abraham and His promises to restore Israel in the future are abundant outside the book of Ezekiel as well. Read the following passages, and again, give a short summary of what each says.

1. Isaiah 43:5-6—

2. Isaiah 60:18-22—

3. Jeremiah 23:5-7—

4. Jeremiah 31:31-34—

5. Amos 9:14-15—

6. Zechariah 8:7-8—

EXECUTE (How does this affect my life?)

1. Because God has been faithful to keep His promises to the children of Israel, we know He will be faithful to keep His promises to His children in the church as well. What do the following passages tell us about God's faithfulness?

   a. 1 John 1:9—

   b. 1 Corinthians 10:13—

c. 1 Thessalonians 5:23-24—

d. 2 Thessalonians 3:3—

2. In Psalm 145:4, David said, "One generation shall praise Your works to another, and shall declare Your mighty acts." He then wrote, "I will declare Your greatness" (verse 6). Based on your own experiences, what can you share with others about God's greatness?

3. Romans 5:7-8 says, "For scarcely for a righteous man will one die; yet perhaps for a good man someone would even dare to die. But God demonstrates His own love toward us, in that while we were still sinners, Christ died for us." What does this tell you about the magnitude of God's love?

4. In what practical ways do we benefit from God's love in our everyday living?

5. In what ways have you gained a greater appreciation for God as you've studied the book of Ezekiel?

CLOSING THOUGHTS

God's faithfulness and love for the people of Israel shone brightly even when they rejected Him. While God's holiness required that He bring judgment against them, at no point did He ever revoke His everlasting promises to them. God does not lie. Every promise He makes, He keeps.

Just as the promises God made to Abraham and his descendants are forever secure, so are the promises God makes to all believers in the church. We never need to worry that God will suddenly and unexpectedly change His mind about our salvation. At the moment we become a new creature in Christ, all our sins—past, present, and future—are forgiven.

What does John 3:16 say is given to "whoever believes in Him"? That person will have "everlasting life." Romans 6:23 describes eternal life as a "gift." If there was no possible way for us to earn salvation, then there is nothing we can do to lose it. Romans 8:1 says, in no uncertain terms, "There is therefore now no condemnation to those who are in Christ Jesus." None!

God is faithful and loving to His own. Yes, there are times when He will find it necessary to discipline or correct us. As Hebrews 12:6 says, "Whom the Lord loves He chastens." And yes, we grieve the Holy Spirit when there is sin in our lives (Ephesians 4:30).

But as Romans 8:38-39 says, "Neither death nor life, nor angels nor principalities nor powers, nor things present nor things to come, nor height nor depth, nor any other created thing, shall be able to separate us from the love of God which is in Christ Jesus our Lord."

Nothing can separate us from God's love and faithfulness.

LESSON 11

THE GREAT EZEKIEL WAR

EZEKIEL 38–39

We now arrive at one of the more remarkable prophecies in the Old Testament that is still future. Through Ezekiel, God warns of a military alliance that will carry out a massive surprise attack against the nation of Israel.

We know this war has not happened yet because the nations that will invade Israel have never fought together before. Ezekiel names the very countries that will rise up against the Jewish nation. When we look at those nations today, we see that they are becoming more connected with one another in a variety of ways—including militarily. We also see that they are primarily made up of Muslim countries that are hostile toward Israel.

There are a number of reasons this prophecy has evoked a lot of curiosity from Christians. One is the timing—Christians are debating whether it will happen before or after the rapture, or closer to the tribulation.

Another is the scale of the invasion. Ezekiel 38 says the enemy "will ascend, coming like a storm, covering the land like a cloud" (verse 9). The clues given by Ezekiel point to a war bigger than any Israel has faced since it became a nation again in 1948.

Then there are the details about how the invaders will be defeated. What the enemy forces thought would be a one-sided battle weighted heavily in their favor will end up crushing them. They won't have a chance.

Through all this, God will once again show His faithfulness to Israel.

Let's go through Ezekiel 38–39 now and see what we can learn about this amazing prophetic event.

CAPTURE THE SCENE (What do I see?)

1. According to Ezekiel 38:2-6, what are the names of the enemy nations that will come against Israel from the north?

2. Read pages 204-206 in *Exploring Ezekiel*. What are the possible evidences for Gog and Magog having a connection to Russia?

3. With help from page 206 of *Exploring Ezekiel*, what other nations will have a part in this alliance?

4. From what direction will this military confederacy originate (verses 6, 15)?

5. Will the attack take place at a time of war or peace, according to Ezekiel 38:8, 11?

6. What does verse 9 tell us about the invasion?

7. What will be one of the enemy's motivations for swooping down into Israel (verses 12-13)?

8. What will some of Israel's neighbors say to the invading forces (verse 13)?

9. What emotions will God exhibit toward the enemy?

10. In what ways will God destroy the invading armies?

11. What will the nations realize at the conclusion of the war?

12. Read Ezekiel 39:4-5. What additional actions will God take against Israel's enemies?

13. After the war, what will the people of Israel do for seven months, and why (verses 11-16)?

14. In general, what does God promise to do with Israel in Ezekiel 39:25-29?

ANALYZE THE MESSAGE (What does it say and mean?)

Using both your Bible and your copy of *Exploring Ezekiel*, answer the following questions.

1. Read Ezekiel 38:4 and 38:16. Who will instigate the enemy nations to rise up and attack Israel? And why (verse 16)?

2. Based on verses 8 and 16, what can we know about the time period during which this war will take place?

3. What specific point does God make about the people of Israel in verses 8 and 12 that informs us this war could not possibly occur before Israel's rebirth in 1948?

4. What evidences do we see in verses 19-22 that indicate the destruction of the enemy forces could only have come from God's hand?

5. What does the fact that Israel will be burning the enemy's weapons for seven years (Ezekiel 39:9) and burying the dead for seven months (verses 12, 14) reveal to us about the extent of the invasion and carnage?

6. In what two significant ways will the relationship between God and Israel take on a new and special dimension, according to Ezekiel 39:29?

COMPARE THIS PASSAGE WITH THE REST OF SCRIPTURE
(How is it supported elsewhere in the Bible?)

Normally in this section of the workbook, we look at other parts of the Bible that *support* the passage we're studying. But in this case, we're going to compare Ezekiel 38–39 with the Gog and Magog event in Revelation 20:8-9 and see how they differ. There are some who believe both passages are talking about the same event. But a careful look reveals that is not the case.

In your copy of *Exploring Ezekiel*, read the section under the subhead "The Timing—Confusion with Revelation 20" on pages 202-203. Below, write a short summary of the three reasons we know these are two completely different wars.

1.

2.

3.

EXECUTE (How does this affect my life?)

1. After God defeats the military alliance that will invade Israel, He explains why He will do this: "Thus I will magnify Myself and sanctify Myself, and I will be known in the eyes of many nations. Then they shall know that I am the LORD" (Ezekiel 38:23).

   God says His purpose will be to make Himself known, to make it clear there is no other explanation for the enemy's defeat. Notice that of all the means God will use to destroy the invading armies (verses 19-22), none involve Israel defending itself with the military prowess that has enabled it to win all the wars it has faced since becoming a nation in 1948.

   Take a moment to recall two or three difficult situations in which God preserved or protected you. What did He do?

2. In what ways have you sensed God protecting you in everyday situations—at home, at work, in school, or in other settings?

3. In Ezekiel 38, God providentially preserved Israel from *physical* warfare. Most of us are more likely to face *spiritual* warfare. What resources or wisdom has God given to us so we can know how to achieve victory in our spiritual battles?

   a. Galatians 5:16—

   b. Ephesians 6:11—

   c. James 4:7—

   d. 1 Peter 5:8—

4. What assurances do we have of God's constant, watchful care?

   a. Psalm 121:7-8—

   b. 2 Thessalonians 3:3—

   c. Hebrews 13:6—

   d. 1 John 4:4—

5. The fact God intervened in the Ezekiel War on Israel's behalf brings to mind what He tells us in Romans 12:19: "Beloved, do not avenge yourselves, but rather give place to wrath; for it is written, 'Vengeance is Mine, I will repay.'"

    As we consider what Romans 12:19 says, keep in mind God's command does not apply to situations where we are justified in taking action to defend ourselves because someone wants to harm us physically, as was the situation for the people of Israel in Ezekiel 38.

    Rather, it's more appropriate for us to apply Romans 12:19 to situations involving hostility, bitterness, anger, and other kinds of negative interactions and treatment with other people. We're far more likely to encounter those kinds of enmity than those that call for physical self-defense.

    With that said, why do you find it a relief to know God will avenge our enemies, and we shouldn't attempt to do so?

6. Romans 12 goes on to say, "If your enemy is hungry, feed him; if he is thirsty, give him a drink; for in so doing you will heap coals of fire on his head. Do not be overcome by evil, but overcome evil with good" (verses 20-21). Why do you think God wants us to show kindness to our enemies? Try to answer this question with both enemies and onlookers in mind.

7. What are some specific ways you can show Christlike love today or very soon to one or two of your enemies?

CLOSING THOUGHTS

There are times when it is extremely difficult to refrain from taking vengeance upon an enemy. We'll find ourselves tempted to plot, in our minds, ways to get back at someone.

Yet Scripture is clear: Vengeance is God's. And Jesus Himself said, "Love your enemies, bless those who curse you, do good to those who hate you, and pray for those who spitefully use you and persecute you" (Matthew 5:44).

Yielding our desire for vengeance up to God is not easy. But we can take comfort in this promise from Him: "Blessed are you when they revile and persecute you, and say all kinds of evil against you falsely for My sake. Rejoice and be exceedingly glad, for great is your reward in heaven, for so they persecuted the prophets who were before you" (Matthew 5:11-12).

God knows what we are enduring. He knows the pain and suffering we face from those who are unkind to us. He is all-seeing and all-knowing, and we aren't. We can know with certainty that He will mete out retribution perfectly, which we're not able to do. And in some way or another—perhaps here on Earth, but most certainly in eternity, we will be rewarded.

Most likely, the vast majority—if not all—of the enemy situations we face in life won't be like the life-threatening warfare Israel faced in Ezekiel 38. But there is one similarity between their predicament and ours: They will end up needing to place their complete trust in God's hands, and we should do the same.

When we do that, we leave room for God to handle the situation His way and to make Himself known. That ensures the best possible outcome.

LESSON 12

THE RETURN OF THE KING

EZEKIEL 40-48

For His beloved prophet Ezekiel, God saved the best for last.

The Lord's servant had done his job willingly, but it had been a long and hard journey.

After so many years of prophesying to a people who had so thoroughly rejected God, he was exhausted. He had faced constant mockery and contempt from those who hadn't wanted to hear the Lord's pronouncements of doom and gloom.

Along the way, Ezekiel had lost his wife. That had left him lonelier than ever. When God had first called him, little had he realized how many painful sacrifices he would endure.

The city of Jerusalem had fallen 14 years earlier and was still in ruins. And the people had been exiled to a foreign land.

Upon turning the page to Ezekiel chapter 40, the change of scenery is dramatic. In a vision, God took the prophet to a high mountain overlooking Jerusalem. What the prophet saw surprised him. Instead of crumbling stonework, there before him stood a glorious temple.

From Ezekiel chapters 1 through 39, condemnation and judgment were the dominant themes. But from chapter 40 onward, promises of restoration and hope shone everywhere.

Because God allowed Ezekiel to prophesy about Israel's future in Christ's glorious kingdom on Earth, the prophet was able to finish his career on a high note. This was an incredible privilege, for God revealed to Ezekiel more details about this coming kingdom than to any other prophet in the Old Testament. Here, we find a wealth of details about what to expect during that amazing era.

But there's also a bit of mystery. What is this business about the measuring rod? And what was this new and expanded edition of the temple all about?

Let's join the prophet and find out.

CAPTURE THE SCENE (What do I see?)

1. Through much of Ezekiel 40–48, we see a lot of measurements being taken. Upon knowing these dimensions, the people would realize this was not one of the past temples, but a different one in the future. What was God wanting to do by revealing these measurements to His people? (For help with the answer, see pages 221-222 in your copy of the book *Exploring Ezekiel*.)

2. What will this new temple communicate about God (see page 223 in *Exploring Ezekiel*)?

3. In contrast to what we read earlier about the glory of the Lord departing from the temple in Ezekiel chapters 9–11, what will happen in this future temple, according to Ezekiel 43:7-9? And for how long?

4. What does Ezekiel 43:26-27 tell us will take place at the millennial temple?

5. What explains the use of the sacrificial system in the millennial temple when Christ already paid the price for our sins at the cross (see page 228 in *Exploring Ezekiel*)?

6. Read Ezekiel 44:1-3 and 45:21-22. There are Bible teachers who say it is possible this prince could be either Jesus or David. But why do we know it cannot be Jesus? (See pages 230-231 in *Exploring Ezekiel*.)

7. Read Ezekiel 47:1-2. What did the prophet see flowing from under the temple?

8. According to Zechariah 14:4, 8, what will cause this water to burst forth?

9. What happened to the water as Ezekiel and his companion walked farther and farther away from the temple (verses 3-5)?

10. What effect will the water have upon nearby riverbanks and the seas that it flows into (verses 7-10, 12)?

11. When God gave the land to the people of Israel, what borders did He specify for that land in Genesis 15:18-21?

12. Has Israel ever fully occupied all that territory (see page 235 in *Exploring Ezekiel*)?

13. What is done to the land in Ezekiel 48:1-29?

14. What will be the name of Jerusalem, according to Ezekiel 48:35?

ANALYZE THE MESSAGE (What does it say and mean?)

Using both your Bible and your copy of *Exploring Ezekiel*, answer the following questions.

1. In Ezekiel 40–48, we read many specific details about the temple, its features and implements, the materials used, instructions for the priests and worship, and more. What does the great exactness of all this tell us about God?

2. Ezekiel 43:13-27 provides specifics about the sacrifices and worship that will take place in the millennial temple. Based on what is said in Hebrews 9:28 and 10:10, how do we know these sacrifices will not be for the purpose of taking away our sins? What will they be meant for instead?

3. During Old Testament history, the intent of the sacrificial system was to point forward to the perfect and final sacrifice offered on the cross, the Savior Jesus Christ. In portions of Ezekiel 40–48, we read about the sacrificial system that will exist during the millennial kingdom, looking back to Christ's sacrifice. While the sacrifices will no longer be needed, why do you think they'll be an important aspect of life during that era? In your answer, consider the purpose of communion. Why do you find communion so special?

4. There are some who say the millennial kingdom is a spiritual, allegorical, or symbolic kingdom. But what actions by Ezekiel and his companion reveal that it is, in fact, a literal and physical kingdom?

COMPARE THIS PASSAGE WITH THE REST OF SCRIPTURE
(How is it supported elsewhere in the Bible?)

There are some who notice certain similarities between Ezekiel 40–48 and Revelation 21–22 and conclude they refer to the same time period in the future.

However, there are distinct differences that make it clear one refers to the millennial kingdom and the other to the eternal state. Read each of the passages below and write down the dissimilarities.

Ezekiel 47:15-20   Revelation 21:1

Ezekiel 48:30-35   Revelation 21:15-17

Ezekiel 47:1   Revelation 22:1

Ezekiel 43:10, 12   Revelation 21:22

EXECUTE (How does this affect my life?)

1. As you consider what you learned about the millennial temple, what stood out to you most, and why?

2. With regard to the past and future temples, God gave instructions for how worship was to be conducted. What do you think God's intent was for giving such guidance?

3. Today, we don't need a temple for worship. We can worship God anywhere at any time. Based on what you understand about worship, what would you say are wrong ways to worship? Right ways?

4. There is coming a day when we will live in a literal, physical, glorious kingdom ruled by Christ. How should an awareness of that shape your life today?

5. Our heavenly Father is in the business of restoration—we see that evident in His relationship with Israel. What are some ways you've experienced God's renewing power in your life?

6. In the millennial kingdom, for the first time ever, we will be ruled by a perfect King. In what ways will living under a divine leader be different from living under human leaders?

7. Based on what you have learned about the millennial kingdom, what are you looking forward to most about it?

8. In your study of the book of Ezekiel, what challenged you most?

9. And what blessed you?

10. In what ways has your appreciation for God grown?

CLOSING THOUGHTS

It's probably safe to say that after Ezekiel had gotten a glimpse of the millennial kingdom, he couldn't wait for it to arrive.

There is coming a day when Israel will be fully restored. The people will dwell in all the land originally promised to Abraham, serve as God's representatives to all the earth, experience God's presence in their midst, and worship and love Him with all their being.

Best of all, the Lord Jesus Christ will rule from David's throne in Jerusalem (1 Chronicles 17:10-14). Under His rule, Israel will prosper as never before. We will see Israel in all its glory.

And that's not all.

There is more to come. After the millennial kingdom will come the eternal state. All God's people will live together in a new heaven and a new Earth. God Himself will dwell with us, and we with Him. There will be no more tears, death, sorrow, nor pain, for they will have passed away. There will be no need for the light of the sun, for the Lord Himself will give light.

God has promised all this and more—all because of His love for us. A love that reached out to us and died on the cross for us even though there was "none...righteous, no, not one; no one understands; no one seeks for God" (Romans 3:10-11).

All through the book of Ezekiel, we have seen God's love, justice, and faithfulness on display to the people of Israel, even when they were at their worst. And today, that same love, justice, and faithfulness is extended to us.

Ezekiel was written so that all might know He is the Lord.

The prophet was faithful to proclaim that truth to his generation. May we likewise be faithful and do the same to ours.

OTHER GREAT HARVEST HOUSE BOOKS
BY AMIR TSARFATI

While the book of Ezekiel was written to the Jews, its prophetic words reveal a strong message of hope for all believers. Discover the peace of knowing that in all situations, God is truly Lord over all.

Bestselling author Amir Tsarfati reveals how Daniel's prophecies—and his unwavering faith amid a contentious culture—provide vital insights for living out these last days with hope and wisdom.

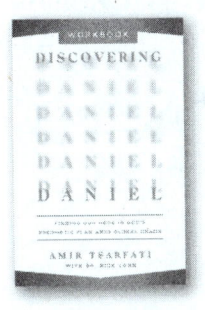

The *Discovering Daniel Workbook* will help you apply the remarkable insights of Daniel to your daily life, emboldening you to live with hope and confidence.

Amir Tsarfati, with Dr. Rick Yohn, examines what Revelation makes known about the end times and beyond. Guided by accessible teaching that lets Scripture speak for itself, you'll see what lies ahead for every person in the end times—either in heaven or on earth. Are *you* ready?

This companion workbook to *Revealing Revelation*—the product of many years of careful research—offers you a clear and exciting overview of God's perfect plan for the future. Inside you'll find principles from the Bible that equip you to better interpret the end-times signs, as well as insights about how Bible prophecy is relevant to your life today.

In *Israel and the Church*, bestselling author and native Israeli Amir Tsarfati helps readers recognize the distinct contemporary and future roles of both the Jewish people and the church, and how together they reveal the character of God and His perfect plan of salvation.

To fully grasp what God has in store for the future, it's vital to understand His promises to Israel. The *Israel and the Church Study Guide* will help you do exactly that, equipping you to explore the Bible's many revelations about what is yet to come.

As a native Israeli of Jewish roots, Amir Tsarfati provides a distinct perspective that weaves biblical history, current events, and Bible prophecy together to shine light on the mysteries about the end times. In *The Day Approaching*, he points to the scriptural evidence that the return of the Lord is imminent.

Jesus Himself revealed the signs that will alert us to the nearness of His return. In *The Day Approaching Study Guide*, you'll have the opportunity to take an up-close look at what those signs are, as well as God's overarching plans for the future, and how those plans affect you today.

Bestselling author and native Israeli Amir Tsarfati provides clarity on what will happen during the tribulation and explains its place in God's timeline.

With this study guide companion to *Has the Tribulation Begun?*, bestselling author and prophecy expert Amir Tsarfati guides you through a biblical overview of the last days, with thought-provoking study and application questions.

AMIR TSARFATI WITH BARRY STAGNER

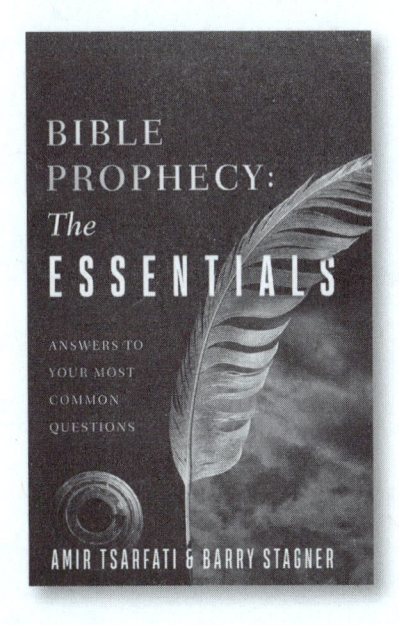

In *Bible Prophecy: The Essentials*, Amir and Barry team up to answer 70 of their most commonly asked questions, which focus on seven foundational themes of Bible prophecy: Israel, the church, the rapture, the tribulation, the millennium, the Great White Throne judgment, and heaven.

AMIR TSARFATI WITH STEVE YOHN

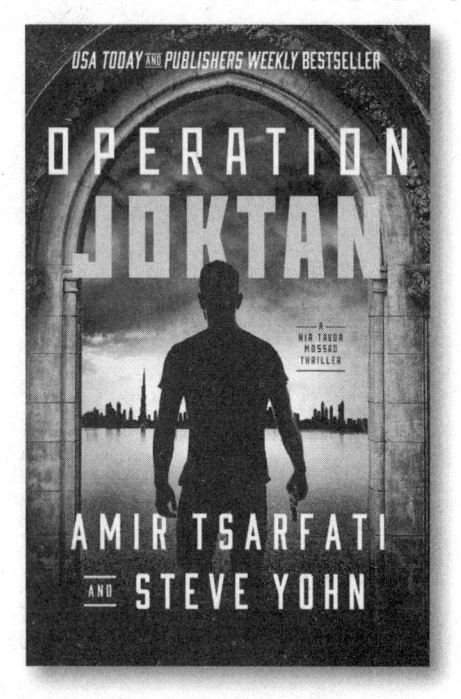

BOOK 1

"It was the perfect day—until the gunfire."

Nir Tavor is an Israeli secret service operative turned talented Mossad agent.

Nicole le Roux is a model with a hidden skill.

A terrorist attack brings them together, and then work forces them apart—until they're unexpectedly called back into each other's lives.

But there's no time for romance. As violent radicals threaten chaos across the Middle East, the two must work together to stop these extremists, pooling Nicole's knack for technology and Nir's adeptness with on-the-ground missions. Each heart-racing step of their operation gets them closer to the truth—and closer to danger.

In this thrilling first book in a new series, authors Amir Tsarfati and Steve Yohn draw on true events as well as tactical insights Amir learned from his time in the Israeli Defense Forces. For believers in God's life-changing promises, *Operation Joktan* is a suspense-filled page-turner that illuminates the blessing Israel is to the world.

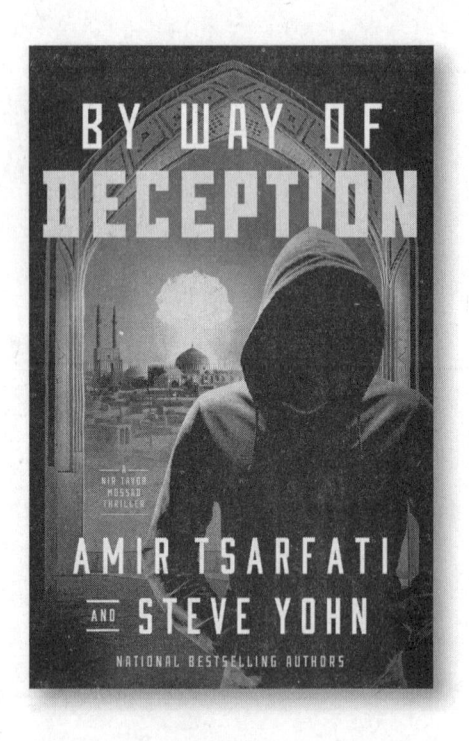

BOOK 2

The Mossad has uncovered Iran's plans to smuggle untraceable weapons of mass destruction into Israel. The clock is ticking, and agents Nir Tavor and Nicole le Roux can't act quickly enough.

Nir and Nicole find themselves caught in a whirlwind plot of assassinations, espionage, and undercover recon, fighting against the clock to stop this threat against the Middle East. As they draw closer to danger—and closer to each other—they find themselves ensnared in a lethal web of secrets. Will they have to sacrifice their own lives to protect the lives of millions?

Inspired by real events, authors Amir Tsarfati and Steve Yohn reteam for this suspenseful follow-up to the bestselling *Operation Joktan*. Filled with danger, romance, and international intrigue, this Nir Tavor thriller reveals breathtaking true insights into the lives and duties of Mossad agents—and delivers a story that will have you on the edge of your seat.

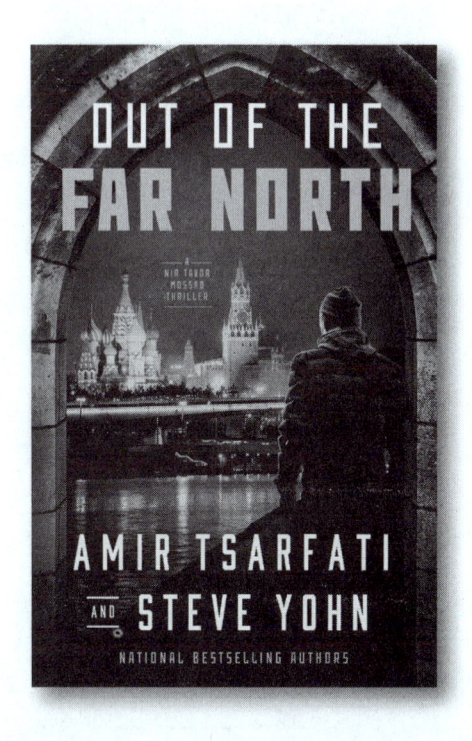

BOOK 3

Tensions are at a breaking point. The Western markets that once relied on Russian gas have turned to Israel for their energy needs. Furious, Russia moves to protect its interests by using its newfound ally, Iran, and Iran's proxy militias.

As Israel's elite fighting forces and the Mossad go undercover, they detect the Kremlin is planning a major attack against Israel. Hunting for clues, Mossad agents Nir Tavor and Nicole le Roux plunge themselves into the treacherous underworld of Russian oligarch money, power, and decadence.

With each danger they face, le Roux's newfound Christian faith grows stronger. And battle-weary Tavor—haunted by dreams from his past—must confront memories and pain he'd sought to bury.

In this electrifying thriller, hostilities explode as Tavor and le Roux fight to prevent a devastating conflict. Will they be able to outwit their enemies, or will their actions have catastrophic consequences?

BOOK 4

After Hamas's brutal massacre against Israel in October 2023, the Mossad embarks on a mission to eliminate the terrorist group's leaders wherever they are.

Tensions escalate as Israel discovers Turkey is harboring Hamas leaders. Despite the Turkish president's warnings, the Mossad guns for these leaders in Turkey and in other parts of the Islamic world. Furious and humiliated by these targeted killings, Turkey's president, backed by Russia and Iran, plans to retaliate by destroying Israel's gas fields with massive drone strikes. Nir Tavor's team is called to action to prevent the attack.

With Israel's energy future at stake and deadly adversaries uniting against the country, Nir and his team face their most dangerous battle for survival against forces determined to see the Jewish nation fall. As Nir's team races against time and relentless foes, an unforeseen global crisis is about to unfold—one that will shock the world and leave Nir reeling and searching for answers.

BEHOLD ISRAEL

Behold Israel is a nonprofit organization founded and led by native Israeli Amir Tsarfati. Its mission is to provide reliable and accurate reporting on developments in Israel and the surrounding region.

Through Behold Israel's website, free app, social media, and teachings in multiple languages, the ministry reaches communities worldwide.

Amir's on-location teachings explain Israel's central role in the Bible and present the truth about current events amidst global media bias against Israel.

FOLLOW US ON SOCIAL

@beholdisrael

BEHOLDISRAEL.ORG

To learn more about our Harvest Prophecy resources, please visit:

www.HarvestProphecyHQ.com

HARVEST PROPHECY
An Imprint of Harvest House Publishers